"A desperate heart cry of the Body of Christ these days has been, 'Where is our discernment?' Thankfully Barbara Wentroble has presented us in this book with a thoughtful and passionate answer. It is good medicine for all of us!"

—**C. Peter Wagner**, presiding apostle,
International Coalition of Apostles

"Many in the Church today have neglected the gift of discernment. Barbara Wentroble has reclaimed this lost gift and is urging us to pick it back up again and use it. I pray the Church is listening to her plea. We must discern the deception that has been sown in our midst and have the boldness to reject the devil's subtle errors. I applaud Barbara for having the courage to write this book in a time when deception is applauded by gullible Christians. God help us to discern truth from error!"

—**J. Lee Grady**, editor, *Charisma* magazine

"These are days of a fresh outpouring of the Holy Spirit. There is an unusual hunger for the supernatural, creating a vulnerability in honest seekers desperate for the supernatural and opening them up to potential deception. It is God whom we desperately need to seek and know in a deeper way. Barbara Wentroble skillfully weaves a tapestry of stories and Scripture, counseling us to recognize 'the veil of deception.' In the last days, deception is one of the main snares we need to guard against. This is a must-read for all honest and passionate God-seekers."

—**Barbara J. Yoder**, senior pastor, author and conference speaker

"Barbara Wentroble has written a much-needed book calling the Body of Christ to higher levels of wisdom and discernment. This is not a book for pastors only but must-reading for every believer. I highly recommend it!"

—**Ché Ahn**, senior pastor, Harvest Rock Church,
Pasadena, Calif.

"Every Christian needs to receive and understand the truths presented in this book."

—**Dr. Bill Hamon**, bishop/apostle, Christian International
Ministries Network (CIMN); author, *Prophets and
Personal Prophecy* and *Day of the Saints*

REMOVING
the VEIL *of*
DECEPTION

REMOVING *the* VEIL *of* DECEPTION

How to Recognize Lying Signs,
False Wonders and Seducing Spirits

BARBARA WENTROBLE

Chosen
a division of Baker Publishing Group
Grand Rapids, Michigan

Published by Chosen Books
a division of Baker Publishing Group
P.O. Box 6287, Grand Rapids, MI 49516-6287
www.chosenbooks.com

Printed in the United States of America

Library of Congress Cataloging-in-Publication Data
Wentroble, Barbara, 1943–
    Removing the veil of deception : how to recognize lying signs, wonders, and seducing spirits / Barbara Wentroble.
      p. cm.
    Includes bibliographical references and index.
    ISBN 978-0-8007-9473-6 (pbk.)
    1. Discernment (Christian theology) I. Title.
BV4509.5W425 2009
234′.13—dc22   2009012254

green
press
INITIATIVE

This book is dedicated to Norma Anderson.
Your love of truth inspires me to search the Scriptures
and to be on the alert against the deception of the enemy.
You have impacted my life and ministry
in a very powerful way!

Contents

Foreword

S piritual discernment is the grace to see into the unseen. It is a gift *of* the Spirit to perceive what is *in* the spirit. Its purpose is to see into the nature of that which is veiled."[1] This quote from Francis Frangipane helps us understand that discernment is something we know by seeing with our spiritual eyes rather than with our physical eyes.

We have entered a season when God's children must increase the power and accuracy of their spiritual discernment on a daily basis. And we have entered a new spiritual realm. We must walk in the Spirit, therefore, to recognize this new realm. It includes human spirits, heavenly spirits (including angels) and demonic hosts. Discerning of spirits is the supernatural gift of the Holy Spirit that allows us to identify the source of the spiritual force influencing an event, circumstance or thought process. Through discernment we develop the strategy of faith and the process of healing necessary to remedy and overcome every problem.

Some in the Body of Christ have the gift of discerning of spirits. Those with a developed, mature gift are able to discern the spiritual atmosphere of a place or around a person. They can do so more often and with more accuracy than most Christians.

I want to make a statement with unwavering confidence: Barbara Wentroble is one who operates in discernment! The Lord could not have chosen anyone better to communicate this subject to the Body of Christ "for a time such as this." *Removing the Veil of Deception* should be one of the staples in every Christian library over the next few decades. This book gives us not only great understanding and examples of spiritual discernment, but practical teaching on how to discern.

Discernment comes through knowing God. To sum up in a few words a long relationship with Barbara Wentroble: She is a woman who knows God. She is known as a prophet and an apostle, a modern-day leader in every sphere of society. I also see her as a life coach. Her discernment helps many find their next step of victory. This book is helpful to anyone, young or old, willing to read it.

The ability to discern spirits is not limited to those with "the gift." God can speak to any Christian through the Holy Spirit and give spiritual insight into any situation. Spiritual discernment may seem complicated or difficult, but it can be as simple as praying until supernatural peace overtakes you. It is really a process of learning how to use the discernment God gives.

There are two main keys to knowing God—through His Word and through hearing, by the spirit, in prayer and intercession (see Hebrews 5:14). Both are important factors in spiritual discernment.

Psalm 119 says, "From Your precepts I get understanding; therefore I hate every false way. Your word is a lamp to my feet and a light to my path" (verses 104–5). As we read and digest the Word of God, we develop important spiritual principles within us. These principles illuminate the path God has for us; they act as a lamp to our feet.

How we process revelation and use our intuition and perception is also very important in walking in spiritual victory. There are certain things we must discern, however, that are not as apparent as the image of an idol. They are spiritual issues and must be discerned spiritually. We must hear from God, in other words, in order to know what is going on. The key to hearing God is prayer—two-way communication in which we speak to Him and He speaks to us.

Hearing the voice of God is not as difficult as some think. I have found that many of God's people are hearing Him but simply not perceiving what they hear as His voice. *To perceive* means "to take hold of, feel, comprehend, grasp mentally, recognize, observe or become aware of something." We must learn to perceive God's voice and the prompting of the Holy Spirit. We must learn to recognize when His Spirit is warning our senses that something evil has invaded our atmosphere.

Have you ever had the hair on your arms and back "stand to attention" when you came into the presence of some object or when you crossed over a boundary into a different atmosphere? That is a form of spiritual discernment. The problem is in knowing what to do.

Through the Word of God, for instance, we understand that we are not to have any carved images of idols in our homes. This understanding helps us become sensitive to seeing carved images of idols all around us, whether in our homes, places of work or wherever we may be. We can gain God's perspective on carved images and idols from His Word. God's Word helped me become aware of all kinds of images around me. This understanding has helped me set a rule about what I will not own—namely, images of idols. In this way, God's Word has become a lamp unto my feet.

From knowing God's Word, then, we can look at objects within our homes and see what does not line up with the Bible. This is part of discernment.

Another aspect of discernment is simply spiritual. Sometimes you just know something is wrong in the environment or atmosphere you have entered. I always tell people, "When the hair on your back and arms stands up, pray until it goes down and you have peace." God can give supernatural revelation to help you know you must take a turn and see something differently.

Some ways God speaks to us are spiritual dreams (dreams that are unusually vivid and detailed and stick in our spirits), visions, visitations, receiving a prophetic word, conversations with friends that bring revelation, messages we have heard or simple "feelings." When we hear from God, we suddenly know that we know something. Revelation has taken place in our spirits. Our challenge is to sharpen our spiritual ears to hear God and not write off what we hear as mere imagination.

God *wants* to communicate with us! We must believe that. Furthermore, He does not want us to be ignorant of how the enemy is trying to ensnare us. He wants to give us discernment to recognize lying signs, wonders and seducing spirits.

Removing the Veil of Deception helps us in both aspects, Word and Spirit, to develop the discernment that will make our walk sure and steady in trying times. Barbara has built a discipleship masterpiece. Read, glean and thresh!

Chuck D. Pierce
President, Glory of Zion International Ministries, Inc.
President, Global Spheres, Inc.

Acknowledgments

No person reaches his or her destiny alone. Writing this book is part of God's destiny for my life. Without the tremendous help from the following people, I could not have reached this goal. Your encouragement and support have made this journey a joy that is beyond words.

My husband, Dale, for your love and ability to see good in me when I am at my worst.

Our adult children, Brian, Lori and Mark. You have always believed in me and made me proud to be your mother.

Our daughters-in-law, Michelle and Britt. You are gifts from the Lord in my life.

Our son-in-law, Brian Kooiman. What a wonderful blessing you are in our family.

Our grandchildren, Lindsey and Annaliese Wentroble; Kailee and Sylvia Wentroble; and Anna, Gabriella and Benjamin Kooiman. I am the most blessed grandparent in the world because of you.

IbM staff: You work tirelessly with enthusiasm over every new project that I launch.

Executive Network members: Your encouragement to write this book helped me continue the process.

Chuck Pierce: You were the first person to see the need for me to write this book. Your prophetic word caused me to jump over every hurdle and accomplish the task.

Jane Campbell, Tim Peterson and the entire staff at Baker Publishing: What a joy to work with a team of people committed to communicating the heart of God in excellence.

Norma Anderson: How can I ever thank you for the many long hours in the night you spent poring over the pages of this manuscript?

Falma Rufus and the IbM Intercessors: Your powerful prayers keep me moving forward.

Finally I want to thank the Lord Jesus Christ for allowing me to be part of the Kingdom of God. You have consumed my heart. You are the passion of my life! May this book be used to bring honor and glory to Your name.

Introduction

W hat am I hearing?" I asked.

The afternoon was to be a time of rest between speaking sessions at a conference. On my way from one of the sessions back to my hotel room, someone had given me a tape. A minister friend was with me, and we had decided to listen to the message while resting.

Rest, however, did not occur that afternoon. Although the words I heard sounded fine in the beginning, it did not take long for me to sense danger. My spirit went on high alert.

The message started out in a solid, biblical way. In fact, I loved what I was hearing. I looked at my friend and commented with a smile, "He must be using some of my notes!"

But within minutes, the message had taken a strange turn. The speaker was telling his listeners that a time would come when the wicked would come out of the place of torment and be reconciled to God. He explained that all, even Satan and his fallen angels, would be held in captivity in hell only for a period of time.

Then the speaker quoted Ephesians 3:21: "To Him be the glory in the church and in Christ Jesus to all generations forever and ever. Amen." He went on to explain that the Greek words for *forever and ever* mean "until the age of the ages." Those who are confined in eternal punishment, he explained, will be held only for a period of time. At the completion of this time, "the age of the ages," everyone will come out of the lake of fire, which is the eternal destiny of the unrighteous awaiting the final judgment.

As the speaker continued with his erroneous doctrine, you could hear excitement growing in the audience. Finally, at the end of the message, the speaker declared, "The time will come when those who are in hell will get so tired of where they are that they will repent." The shouting and applause were deafening.

"Even the devil will get saved!" he continued. "Just think about this—everyone you have ever prayed for will eventually be saved!"

The audience continued its thunderous applause, clapping and shouting. The listening ears had heard what they wanted to hear. All their loved ones, everyone—including rebellious friends, drug addicts, murderers, fornicators and child molesters—would get tired of hell and be converted.

Not only these unrighteous ones but the devil himself would be saved!

On an afternoon when I was trying to relax, I felt shocked, and started thanking the Lord for my biblical foundation. I realized more than ever how important basic principles are to the believer. For example:

Therefore leaving the elementary teaching about the Christ, let us press on to maturity, not laying again a foundation of repentance from dead works and of faith toward God.

Hebrews 6:1

Because of my foundation in the Word of God and the sensitivity in my spirit, I was protected from the message I had just heard. But the enticing words had had a powerful appeal. Greek and Hebrew words had been used, ostensibly to credential the teaching. Without a biblical foundation, it would have been easy to be swept up in the charisma and finely structured doctrine—historically known as ultimate reconciliation—of the speaker.

The impact of the taped message that day forever changed my life. From that time, I began a journey to guard against deception in the Body of Christ. I asked the Lord to sensitize my mind and spirit to wrong doctrines that might lead me and others away from God's truth in His Word.

Years later another high-profile minister released a similar doctrine. He had changed his theology after establishing a successful and influential ministry. Long-time associates and friends seemed shocked as he announced his endorsement of an unusual, separate "gospel" affecting sincere but uninformed believers.

Here are some of the tenets of this doctrine, generally recognized as the gospel of inclusion:

- Jesus' death on the cross and His resurrection paid the price for all humanity to enjoy eternal life in heaven, without any requirement to repent of sins and receive salvation.
- Belief in Jesus Christ is not necessary for a person to go to heaven. Salvation is unconditional, granted by the grace of God to every human being.
- All humanity will go to heaven regardless of religious affiliation, even those who believe in false religions or who adopt any alternate form of religious persuasion or who have no religious persuasion at all. In heaven all humanity will be in harmony with the Kingdom of God.
- Only those who have tasted the fruits of real intimacy with Christ *and have intentionally and consciously rejected the grace of God* will spend eternity separated from God.
- Some people will experience some type of hell, but it is important to get away from the picture of an angry, intolerant God.
- The Bible is the inspired word of man, about God.

I wish I could say that the above examples are the only areas of deception today in the Body of Christ. These are only a few examples of deceptive traps that are ensnaring millions of believers. Voices are being raised that proclaim a different gospel, coupled with "signs" such as bleeding hands, tears on the faces of statues and other spiritual manifestations too numerous to mention. Voices must be raised to counteract the error. This is not a time to be politically correct but to remove the veil of deception from the minds and spirits of God's people.

I do not think for a minute that I am the only voice speaking on this topic. Nor do I claim to be a theologian or expert in the area of deception. Nor can I address such a huge subject completely in one book. Yet I must sound the alarm. I cannot keep silent.

I pray that the content of this book will cause you to be a Berean believer: "more noble-minded than those in Thessalonica, for they received the word with great eagerness, examining the Scriptures daily to see whether these things were so" (Acts 17:11). I pray that you will not follow every wind of doctrine that blows through the Church, but search the Scriptures diligently to see if the things you are seeing and hearing are from the Spirit of God.

May the Lord quicken your mind and spirit with the purpose of leading you into all truth.

1

Living in Perilous Times

But know this, that in the last days perilous times will come.

2 Timothy 3:1, NKJV

Watching TV has never been something I particularly enjoy. If I turn on the set, I usually watch the news in order to know how to pray. Sometimes I check the Weather Channel to see what clothes I need to pack for a trip. But I do remember watching a few programs during my growing-up years. One of the popular programs during that time was *Bewitched*.

The actress Elizabeth Montgomery played the role of a cute blonde witch named Samantha. When Samantha wanted something to happen, she simply twitched her nose and it happened.

To the uninformed—which included me—the program seemed endearing and amusing. Receiving the highest ratings ever for the network, it enjoyed an eight-year run from 1964 to 1972. Elizabeth Montgomery received five Emmy Awards and four Golden Globe nominations for her role in what was considered a sophisticated sitcom. As for Samantha, with her on-screen magic and famous nose twitch, she became a role model for millions.

Years later, television made the occult even more attractive. The "beautiful people" were invited to call the local station and get their psychic readings. It sounded fun and encouraging. These programs were not dark and gloomy and frightening. They were entertaining and seemingly innocent.

One time I turned on the TV to find a woman going into a trance and "prophesying." Her words were so lengthy and confusing that the host of the show finally had to help her snap out of the trance so he could end the program.

During this era, the nation's military ventures began to fail. President John Kennedy was assassinated. Large numbers of young people revolted against authority and began to abuse drugs. Education standards declined. The economy became unstable.

In 1982 George Anderson became the first medium in the United States to have a weekly television program. That show, *Psychic Channels*, began to change the way people perceived mediums (people who convey messages between the dead and the living). Anderson's program created a path for other psychic shows to be accepted. In 2001 he appeared on a series of specials called *Contact: Talking to the Dead*.

What was happening? A subtle shift was taking place in people's minds.

The history of the United States reveals a people who have paid lip service, at the very least, to Christian principles. The founding fathers covenanted that this new nation would honor God. They desired the protection of religious rights for every individual. No one was forced to adhere to a certain faith. The American legal system could not compel a citizen to believe or worship in a certain way. These forefathers encouraged public prayer, spiritual holidays and a strong belief in a loving and kind Creator.

But a subtle change has taken place. I appreciate Peter Marshall and David Manuel's description of this change in their book *The Light and the Glory*:

> Perhaps the most mystifying indicator of all was the loss of moral soundness. To be sure, there had always been pockets of dissolution, but we had thought of them as isolated situations—surface cavities which needed to be drilled and filled. Now we were finding that what was actually needed was root-canal work, if it was not already too late.[1]

The Bible warns us of times like this:

> Know this, that in the last days perilous times will come . . . [with men] having a form of godliness but denying its power. And from such people turn away! . . . But evil men and impostors will grow worse and worse, deceiving and being deceived.
>
> 2 Timothy 3:1, 5, 13, NKJV

That New King James word *perilous* means "dangerous." The times are dangerous due to the deception that abounds.

It is easy to understand non-Christians being deceived and influenced by evil. The problem is when we find Christians and even church leaders who are deceived. Often the mindsets of people who once walked in the truth of God's Word have changed. As a result they open themselves to doctrines and spiritual manifestations that are not biblically sound.

How does this happen? And how can you and I keep our own minds free from deception?

How Can We Protect Ourselves?

We will be looking, in the course of this book, at many important ways we can steer clear of deception and walk in purity in the presence and power of God. But let's look first at three fundamental protections.

The Foundation of God's Word

When it comes to having a mind free from deception, there is no substitute for immersing ourselves in the Word of God. Too often in our churches we hear lots of wonderful music, enthusiastic preaching and sermons that make us feel good. But most people who call themselves believers, according to polls, do not know the most fundamental truths of the Bible. Frequently churchgoers do not even have a biblical worldview and live their lives separate from truths found in the Bible.

A person needs to be fed the Word of God in order to grow into maturity. God's Word is the diet that brings us to spiritual maturity. Physical food can never satisfy the deep longing inside for satisfaction. Only God's Word can do this.

Although I grew up in church, I did not read my Bible unless I was attending a church service. As a child in Sunday school, I did not understand why I needed to read my Bible each day. The only benefit I thought I would receive was the check mark on my offering envelope that gave me ten percent of the requirements needed to earn a grade of one hundred percent. It was easy to go to church on time, give an offering, listen to the pastor preach and do a few other required things. By performing those quick tasks, I could earn a total score of ninety percent. Why should I spend an entire week reading my Bible to receive only ten percent more? After all, ninety percent wasn't too bad.

How little I understood the necessity of having a foundation built on God's Word in my life!

The church I attended as I was growing up said it believed the entire Bible. Yet each year we spent a month learning what our *denomination* believed. By the time I reached adulthood, I did not know the simple truths of the Word of God, even though I had spent all those years in church. I had heard about a man named Paul but did not know if he was in the Old Testament or the New Testament. I heard about Moses but could not have found him in the Bible if my life depended on it.

Attending church services and hearing sermons is no guarantee that a person is grounded in the Word of God!

Recently a prominent preacher was interviewed on TV. He was asked, "Do you believe Muslims and Jews are going to hell?" His response shocked me. "I don't know," he replied. "We don't talk about hell."

Any young Christian should be able to answer this question after attending a new believers' class. Hell is taught in Scripture—most of all by Jesus Himself. The Lord Jesus died in our place so no one would have to go to hell. But sinners choose this place of separation from God when they reject the provision of His Son.

Is it any surprise that believers are prone to deception when our leaders refuse to answer a foundational question like this with a biblical response? Without being grounded in the truth of God's Word, it is easy for minds to be swayed toward deception.

One of the first things that happened to me after receiving the fullness of the Holy Spirit was an insatiable desire for the Word of God. I spent hours each day reading and studying the Scriptures. The Bible came alive to me, and I saw and understood things I had never comprehended before. Although I had gone to church all my life, I had never been able to grasp the secrets found in the Word. Now I had an open treasure box with the riches of God freely available to me. I loved it![2]

For the past twenty years I have made a practice of reading through the Bible each year. I am not suggesting a religious ritual, but a discipline that keeps our spirits alive and well nourished. A spirit full of the Word of God will help guard against the deception of the enemy.

The Leading of God's Spirit

Not only do we need the Word of God to help guard us against deception, we also need the power of the Holy Spirit. God gives His Spirit to dwell in us and to empower us to live victorious lives.

Jesus promised His disciples on the night before He was crucified that the Holy Spirit would be not only *with* them but *in* them (see John 14:17). He continued by telling them that this Holy Spirit "will teach you all things, and bring to your remembrance all that I said to you" (verse 26). The Holy Spirit gives our spirits a nudge so we can avoid deception.

How many times in life have I missed listening to the quickening of the Holy Spirit? Looking back on some situations, I can remember the nudging of the Spirit, but I let my brain or thinking processes get in the way of His leading. Overriding the voice of the Holy Spirit in those situations left me vulnerable to the snares of the enemy.

A few times I have bought something or made a financial investment that I felt a nudge in my spirit not to. Somehow I reasoned away the gentle leading of the Holy Spirit and convinced myself that I should buy the product or make the investment. Later the decision turned out to be wrong. It may seem to be a small thing, but God was teaching me to hear and obey His voice. He wanted me to be led by His Spirit so I would be prepared for greater dangers in the days ahead.

Keeping an Inquiring Mind

Another way to avoid deception is by keeping your mind active. Allowing it to shift into neutral is not a sign of spirituality. Certain charismatic teachers have implied that rational thinking is unspiritual and carnal and that they, not their followers, are the ones to examine a new doctrine or teaching. If someone questions a visitation of Jesus or the appearance of an angel or some other supernatural occurrence, then the person questioning must be in unbelief and actually rebelling against the Lord.

But the Holy Spirit does not come to take your brain away. He actually gives you an inquiring mind full of the wisdom of God. Although we are to surrender our wills to the Lord, we continue to do His will by the active choice of our minds. We were not created to be robots. God wants us to cooperate with His Spirit by using every part of our being—body, soul (including the mind) and spirit. God desires His creatures to be thinking, rational, renewed persons made after His own image.

Deceivers sometimes use the Word of God to try to get their listeners to throw away reason and scrutiny of doctrines or supernatural phenomena. Usually these deceivers will quote a Scripture such as 1 Corinthians 2:14: "A natural man does not accept the things of the Spirit of God, for they are foolishness to him; and he cannot understand them, because they are spiritually appraised." Implied is this: If you do not embrace the manifestation or doctrine that is occurring, you are "in the flesh," resisting the anointing of the Holy Spirit.

Everything supernatural, however, is not from God, nor is everything that appears to be supernatural that happens inside church buildings.

An Issachar Anointing

The danger of deception is not new in the world. We see instances of deception throughout the Bible. Satan is revealed from Genesis to Revelation as the deceiver. He took advantage of the first created humans and their highest and purest desires toward God. He cloaked his trickery with the lure of making Adam and Eve wise—to be like God. The serpent's promise blinded them to the obedience that is always required for us to draw near to God.

Satan thought he won the victory in the Garden of Eden. He did not understand the power of God that would eventually destroy his short-lived victory.

Throughout the Old Testament we read about instances of deception. This pattern of the evil schemes of the enemy against God's people continues through the New Testament. Jesus, "the last Adam" (1 Corinthians 15:45), stepped onto the scene to destroy the works of Satan. The first Adam was tested in the Garden of Eden. The last Adam received a corresponding testing in the wilderness of Judea. Although Satan was able to deceive and institute rebellion against God through the first Adam, his evil deception was conquered by the last Adam.

Even though Jesus conquered the deceiver, we find the same problem of deception in the powerful infant Church. Paul asked the Galatian believers, "Who has bewitched you?" (see Galatians 3:1).

The word *bewitched*—just where we started this chapter!—comes from the Greek word *baskaino*, meaning "to cast a spell on someone." A type of demonic spell had been cast on the believers in Galatia. Paul called the teaching used to cast this spell "another gospel" (Galatians 1:6, KJV).

Not only are unregenerate men and women deceived, but even Christians—in this case, the Galatian believers—can be deceived. Jesus prophesied that "false Christs and false prophets will arise, and will show signs and wonders, in order to lead astray, if possible, the elect" (Mark 13:22). Understanding that Christians are not exempt from deception alerts us to the reality of 2 Timothy 3:1—that we are living in "perilous times" (NKJV).

The "times" spoken about in that verse is the Greek word *kairos*. This word carries with it the meaning of a strategic time, an opportune moment. The fact is, we are living in strategic times for the Lord's purposes to be released in the earth. But at the same time, the enemy is roaming about seeking to deceive and devour God's people through deception. He senses that this is an opportune time for him to lead God's people astray.

Jesus admonished His disciples for understanding physical weather yet not discerning these *kairos* times:

> "When it is evening, you say, 'It will be fair weather, for the sky is red.' And in the morning, 'There will be a storm today, for the sky is red and threatening.' Do you know how to discern the appearance of the sky, but cannot discern the signs of the times?"
>
> Matthew 16:2–3

Too often we resemble the New Testament disciples. We should be like the modern meteorologists who are able to understand natural weather patterns days before they happen. Yet often we cannot discern the perilous times we are living in. Our greatest danger is not disease and plague, although there are terrible afflictions in the world. Our greatest danger is not poverty and corruption, even though these also cause much suffering. Our greatest danger today is not even war and terrorism, although these are treacherous realities. Our greatest danger is deception, which is able to keep God's people from His highest and best for their lives and for eternity.

Listen to the admonition of Paul:

> We are no longer to be children, tossed here and there by waves and carried about by every wind of doctrine, by the trickery of men, by craftiness in deceitful scheming.
>
> Ephesians 4:14, NKJV

We are living at a time when many winds of doctrine are blowing through the Church. Let's be people who will arise with the Issachar anointing and catch God's wind to go where He wants to take us, rather than be blown in the wrong direction.

We need to be a company of people like "the sons of Issachar, men who understood the times, with knowledge of what Israel should do" (1 Chronicles 12:32). These men understood the strategic, opportune times of the Lord. They had the wisdom of God to discern the times they were living in and to know what they should do during those times.

Several years ago I spent a few days in Switzerland. On one of those days in that beautiful land, I went with a couple of friends to the top of a magnificent mountain. While we stood looking out over the vast expanse of the Alps, I noticed a man and woman near the summit with hang gliders. From time to time they would put their hands out and check the wind currents. Finally the strategic time came. As I watched in amazement, the couple mounted their hang gliders and were carried off by the wind. They directed their gliders carefully around the mountains until they were out of sight.

How did they know when to take off? Were they discerning the right time when they put their hands out into the wind? Did they need the wind to blow in a certain direction for them to succeed in reaching their destination?

Somehow I felt they were trained to know how to discern natural wind. They could not take off when just any wind was blowing. They sensed the right wind and the right time. They needed skill to be successful and reach their destination.

You and I should be the same way. We need training to exercise our senses to discern good and evil:

> Solid food is for the mature, who by constant use have trained themselves to distinguish good from evil.
>
> Hebrews 5:14, NIV

My friend Barbara Murrell had an open vision in the early 1990s in which she heard a knock at her door. The being she saw as she opened the door greeted her by saying, "I am the spirit of Truth and I have come to visit you." Later she saw another being who announced that he was the spirit of Grace. The Lord told her that she would experience Truth and Grace coming together.

As Barbara was ready to close the door, she noticed three other beings in her yard. These beings were spirits named Lying, Seducing and Deceiving. *Where you see one of the spirits*, the Lord told her, *you see all three.*

As she closed the door, the Lord told her that if she had rejected Truth, she would have opened her house to those three spirits. And He exhorted her to use her greatest weapon during these days: the weapon of Truth.

How we need truth as protection against the lying, seducing and deceiving spirits sent to destroy God's people! No longer can we afford to be spiritual babies blown around by winds of false teaching.

Along with solid biblical food, we must have the anointing that the sons of Issachar had so we can discern the perilous times we are living in. Only then will we know what we are to do. Only as we are trained and anointed by the Holy Spirit for this time in history can we follow the Lord into His highest and best for our lives.

The Bible exhorts us not to be deceived. God wants us to be steadfast in our faith and not tossed around by every wind of doctrine. In this age when supernatural power is promoted by evil influencers, we need to be the sons of Issachar.

In the next chapter we will discover some of the tools God has given the Church to keep us from deception.

Prayer

Father, I want to walk in freedom from deception and serve You faithfully all the days of my life. I ask You to cause me to be alert in my spirit and able to guard against any form of deception. I choose to have a mind that is alert and renewed by Your Word. I ask You, Lord, to give me an Issachar anointing so that I may sense the strategic time I am living in and know what You are saying for this season. Thank You, Lord, for helping me to know truth so that I may live in the freedom You have provided for me. In Jesus' name, Amen.

For Further Reflection

1. In what ways are we being deceived by a changing culture?
2. What are some of the ways we can keep our minds free from deception?
3. Was there a time when you missed the leading of the Holy Spirit?
4. What lessons did you learn from that experience?
5. What are some ways you can develop the Issachar anointing in your own life?

2

Be Not Deceived

The road trip would take about four hours before I reached the conference center where I would be speaking. How relaxing to get out of city traffic while driving on a long stretch of highway! I suddenly remembered a tape I had received from the elders of my church. They were considering asking the speaker on the tape to come to our church. They wanted me to listen to the message and see if I felt right about having him minister to our congregation.

After popping the tape into the player, I listened intently. The doctrine was solid. It was a great message! Since it was so powerful, it seemed right to invite this man to speak. But something inside me did not feel right.

I am not the kind of person who relies on feelings for most decisions. As a leader, I am aware that feelings can lead a person in the wrong direction. And at that time in my life, I was learning how to discern the difference between *feelings* and the *voice of the Holy Spirit.*

So what was wrong?

After returning home, I talked with the elders. I let them know that the message on the tape sounded great. It was biblically sound and encouraging and would be a wonderful message for our congregation. Yet something still seemed wrong. I could not explain it.

After listening to my concerns, the elders decided not to invite the man since I could not sense a green light in my spirit.

Several months later we heard that the man had left his wife and run away with his secretary. Things had been taking place while the elders were deciding whether or not he should minister to our church. Unfortunately, my uneasy feelings had been confirmed, even though we were unaware of the man's activities at the time. I learned a very valuable lesson. *Do not override the leading of the Holy Spirit.*

How thankful I am for the Spirit of God! In these perilous times—which we discussed in the last chapter—God has given us His Spirit to lead, guide and caution us about the deceptive snares of the enemy.

Jesus warned His disciples about deception in the Olivet discourse in Matthew 24. The disciples were asking Him what would be happening and what signs would be displayed indicating His coming and the end of the world. Jesus replied in a very interesting way. He did not give a direct answer. He simply said,

> "Take heed that no one deceives you. For many will come in My name, saying, 'I am the Christ,' and will deceive many. . . . Many false prophets will rise up and deceive many. . . . False christs and false prophets will arise and show great signs and wonders so as to deceive, if possible, even the elect."
>
> verses 4–5, 11, 24, NKJV

Amazing! The Bible says that even God's elect, His chosen ones, can be deceived. Even maturity is no guarantee as a shield against this evil.

What, then, is deception? A misrepresentation of the facts. Deception means to mislead someone or make that person believe certain facts or situations that are not true. Even though that person may love the Lord, the enemy can pull the wool over his or her spiritual eyes.

According to the prophet Jeremiah, "the heart is more deceitful than all else and is desperately sick" (17:9). The word *deceitful* comes from a root word that describes a hill or uneven place.[1] This terrain can prevent people from moving forward. Deception is a tactic of the enemy that keeps unregenerate man—anyone who has not turned to Jesus for forgiveness of sin—from arising into the full purpose God has planned for his or her life.

Sin is deceitful, according to Hebrews 3:13, and hardens a person's heart toward the Lord and toward His plan for that person's life. When the person's heart becomes hardened, it gives entrance to "the god of this world" to blind his or her mind (2 Corinthians 4:4). Only as the light of God's Word and Spirit penetrate this blinded mind can the person be set free.

The fact that a person has been living a Christian lifestyle is no guarantee that he or she is free from the power of deception. In fact, the stronger a Christian's walk with the Lord, the more subtle the tactics of the enemy. Satan's strategy is to entice believers away from truth.

The Gift of Discernment

Sandy experienced the pain of these subtle tactics of the enemy. She grew up as the adopted daughter of a preacher. He abused her sexually throughout her childhood. During these times, he would tell her that she was God's gift to him. He was deceived into believing that God had brought this little girl into his life for his own perverted pleasure. Talk about deception!

But God has an answer for deception, which Sandy learned as she grew older. He gave Christians a gift called the "discerning of spirits" (1 Corinthians 12:10, NKJV). The word *discerning* carries with it the meaning of distinguishing or separating good from evil.

Four types of discernment are available to help us in our Christian walk.

Natural Discernment

The first type is natural discernment, which belongs to both Christians and non-Christians. This is what we use when we pass judgment on people, on circumstances or on our own behavior. When a man is angry and kicks the tires on his car, we say he is carnal or childish. We are observing his actions and using natural discernment.

We derive the content of our judgment, in part, from teachings we received as we were growing up. It is also the result of environment and culture.

Some actions are acceptable in one culture but not in another. My father had a difficult time accepting a man wearing a hat indoors. Dad's mother was British and taught him that wearing hats indoors was not correct. Today men and boys wear baseball caps and other headgear indoors as well as outdoors. But since my father grew up with a different cultural norm, his natural discernment told him that this practice was wrong.

This type of discernment, then, is for practical as well as spiritual truth. The world uses this type of discernment as a basis for making decisions. Natural discernment also supplies much of the content of our consciences. But since it can be an unreliable resource, we must look to a different method if we are to discern truth.

Intellectual Discernment

Another type of discernment is intellectual discernment, given to us when we have minds that have been renewed in Jesus Christ. Our intellectual discernment grows as we come to know the Lord and His Word in a deeper way.

Everyone who partakes only of milk is not accustomed to the word of righteousness, for he is an infant. But solid food is for the mature, who because of practice have their senses trained to discern good and evil.

Hebrews 5:13–14

The "senses" referred to in that passage are really our perceptions or judgments. As we mature in our walk with the Lord, we are able to recognize actions and circumstances that are not characteristic of truth. People trained in handling money study genuine currency so much that they can easily recognize counterfeit bills. In the same way, believers should meditate on biblical truth to such a degree that we can identify spiritual counterfeits.

False Supernatural Discernment

Another type of discernment, false supernatural discernment, causes a demonically influenced person to be antagonistic toward the presence of God or His people. A person involved in satanic activity will often be repelled by anyone walking in the Spirit.

A visitor came to our church while my husband, Dale, and I were pastoring. The woman could not stay for more than a few minutes during the service. She felt so uncomfortable that she actually ran out of the building. Although she was a believer, she had been involved in occult activity before her conversion and discerned the presence of God in the meetings. Later she went to a deliverance counselor and was rescued from the demonic influences controlling her. Then she was able to enjoy church services and the presence of God.

Discerning of Spirits

The fourth type of discernment is the discerning of spirits, a gift that the Lord gives His people. This type of discernment provides insight into the spirit world and enables believers to make judgments in regard to spirits that are either good or evil. (Often people will say the Lord has given them a gift of discernment. The supernatural gift that the Lord gives, however, is not *discernment* but rather *the discerning of spirits.*)

The discerning of spirits has no relationship to natural discernment.

- It is not metaphysical in its operation. Spiritual metaphysics uses various disciplines and exercises to awaken and unfold faculties and virtues that are supposedly the divinity within.
- The discerning of spirits is not necromancy (communicating with the dead).
- It is not psychoanalysis or extrasensory perception (ESP).
- It is not thought reading. In fact, this gift has nothing to do with the realm of the mind at all. It is not discernment of *things* but of *spirits.*

I knew a woman who felt she was highly gifted in the discerning of spirits. The problem was, she could see only those things in a person's life that were wrong. She could never acknowledge anything good in that person. Rather than having the discerning of spirits, I think she had the gift of suspicion!

Discerning Spirit Beings

Not only are there several methods of discerning, but there are dissimilar kinds of spirits that need to be discerned. Human beings cannot be in contact with or understand the reality of the spiritual realm apart from the power of God or the power of Satan. The spirit world is as genuine and varied as the physical world, but the various spiritual beings can be discerned with accuracy only as we are taught by the Holy Spirit (see 1 Corinthians 2:14–15).

We find spirit beings in several different categories. I will mention five: God, angelic beings, humans, demonic beings and the devil.

38

Believers need the ability to distinguish one from another in each of these categories. There are more spirit beings than we will look at here, but for the purposes of this book, let's look at five kinds of spirits.

God as Spirit

The first thing to understand is that "God is spirit, and those who worship Him must worship in spirit and truth" (John 4:24). In other words, our worship of God should come from our spirits and not just from our minds. Although we cannot see Him, we can learn to recognize His presence and commune with Him spirit to Spirit.

As I indicated in the last chapter, I grew up in a traditional church where I was taught about the power and presence of God without ever experiencing these. In fact, I never knew anyone who had experienced God's power personally. Only after my own supernatural encounter with the Holy Spirit was I able to really worship God as Spirit—in spirit and in truth.

The Human Spirit

Not only is God Spirit, but human beings are spirit, too (see Job 32:8). God is able to give us understanding of things beyond our human knowledge. He speaks to our spirits and tells us things that our minds have not learned. As He does, we are able to tap into His wisdom. If we are to experience life in its fullness, we need our spirits to be awakened by the Holy Spirit.

Before we are born again, we are like corpses walking around! Our bodies are alive but our spirits are dead (see James 2:26). At the time of salvation our spirits are made alive. We now have the ability to communicate with the Lord and relate to Him in a supernatural way, spirit to Spirit. We experience satisfaction in life when we hear the voice of the Lord speaking to our spirits, as I wrote about in *Prophetic Intercession*:

We are called the sheep of His pasture and have the privilege of hearing the voice of the Good Shepherd. What a promise! God is not so busy holding stars in space, keeping galaxies on their course or causing this earth to spin on its axis that He doesn't have time to talk to you and me. He even gives us assurance that we will know the difference between His voice and the other voices that may speak to us.[2]

Angelic Beings

Angels are another form of spirit beings. The Bible abounds with events in which angels were involved, and describes angelic beings such as cherubim and seraphim. God has provided angels to assist His followers in their tasks on earth. But Western culture often overlooks the power of these beings:

Modern man often denies the existence and operation of angels on Earth. Many today believe, like the deists, that God created the universe billions of years ago. They also believe that He wound the world up like a clock and then left it to run by itself. The doctrine of deism is that God created the world and its natural laws but refrains from intervening in history with miracles or making any alteration to the natural order.

The Bible does not teach this concept. It teaches that *God is intimately involved in running the universe all the time.* . . .

Although God is intimately involved in running the universe at all times, He sometimes uses angels to assist in the running of the world. These angels are perfect servants to God; therefore, they are models for us to follow as God's servants on Earth.[3]

Demonic Beings

Although God has made His angelic spirits available to believers, there are also demons, as well as a hierarchy of thrones, dominions, principalities and powers. Believers cannot use natural discernment to recognize any of these. We must operate in the true gift of the discerning of spirits to recognize their influence and to be protected from the deception these evil beings bring to people and situations and even entire regions.

One theory is that what we know as demonic spirits or demons may have been part of the great rebellion that took place in heaven:

> They are spirits of demons, performing signs, which go out to the kings of the whole world, to gather them together for the war of the great day of God, the Almighty.
>
> Revelation 16:14

There are differences of opinion on the origin of demons and fallen angels. But whatever their origin, evil spirits and their demonic rulers, cast out of heaven, now seek to gain control in the earth. These evil beings are under the authority of Satan and do his bidding.

The Devil

Second Corinthians 11:14 teaches that "Satan himself masquerades as an angel of light" (NIV). Before we were born again, we lived under the rulership of "the prince of the power of the air" (Ephesians 2:2). He controlled our lives when we were sons of disobedience, even when we failed to recognize his influence. Our eyes were blind and could not see the destruction he was bringing into our lives. We were deceived!

Unlocking Your Spiritual Gifts

But God is faithful to give us the discerning of spirits to help us recognize the spirit beings that surround us. Ask Him to unlock the spiritual gifts that belong to you as His follower. Don't be intimidated by those who accuse you when you discern a wrong spirit. It may be that a deceived or false leader will accuse you of being "an old wineskin" when you will not blindly follow those operating under the influence of wrong spirits.

Regardless of the pressure you receive, stand strong in your convictions. Search the Scriptures, fast, pray and allow the Holy Spirit to guide you.

In the next chapter we will look at some of the deceptive practices designed to lead you away from the path of the Lord.

Prayer

Heavenly Father, thank You for giving me the supernatural ability to discern spirits. I ask You to sharpen the gift of discerning of spirits in my life. Help me be sensitive to the leading of Your Holy Spirit so I do not miss what You are saying to me. Place a hunger within me for Your Word. I long to be led by Your Holy Spirit into all truth. With Your help, Lord, I want to walk free from deception all the days of my life. Thank You for leading me and for enabling my spirit to hear what Your Spirit is saying to me. In Jesus' name I pray, Amen.

For Further Reflection

1. Was there a time you sensed something wrong without having proof that something actually *was* wrong? What happened?
2. Give your own definition of *deception*.
3. Give your own definition of *discerning*.
4. Describe the four types of discernment.
5. What are the five different types of spirits we discussed?
6. How would you respond if you were accused of being "an old wineskin" after refusing to go against the discernment God had given you?

3

Lying Signs, Wonders and Apparitions

Years ago I was invited to speak at a conference in southern Louisiana. After arriving for the event, I was informed that this was a special time for that area. Some of the churches were showing videos taken in the small village of Medjugorje located in Bosnia-Herzegovina. These videos showed what they claimed was the blessed virgin Mary appearing in the sky.

Six young people in the village who started seeing the apparition in 1981 were called the visionaries. Each of them was promised ten secrets concerning the future, to be received from impressions transmitted by the apparition. When each visionary has received all ten secrets, the apparition will stop appearing to that person every day. Since the appearances began, millions of people from all faiths, from all over the world, have visited Medjugorje to see the virgin Mary. Currently only three visionaries have reported receiving all ten messages, but none has fully disclosed them. The Catholic Church has not authorized devotion to "Our Lady of Medjugorje" and, according to the Vatican website in early 2009, "appearances in this village have not yet been officially recognized by the Church authorities."

During the time I was in Louisiana, some of the churches encouraged their congregants to wait outside their homes on a certain day. (The conference where I was ministering was not part of this group.) The people were given the time when the virgin Mary from Medjugorje would appear in the sky. Sure enough, at that time, the people stood outside gazing heavenward to view the appearance they were promised.

My heart went out to these people as they gazed up into the sky. They were hungry for a supernatural visitation from God. How disappointed they must have been when the apparition failed to appear! They and the leaders who encouraged them were deceived in their quest for supernatural phenomena.

The fact that churchgoers can be deceived is grievous. It is one thing for unbelievers to be deceived. It is even more grievous when spiritual leaders are deceived.

A similar example of an apparition is "Our Lady of Guadalupe" in Mexico. The brown-skinned virgin who is said to have appeared in the sixteenth century is Mexico's most beloved religious and cultural image and a significant role model for the Mexican identity. The Basilica of Our Lady of Guadalupe in Mexico City is the second-most-visited Roman Catholic shrine in the world (after St. Peter's Basilica within Vatican City).

From time to time we see reports on TV about statues that cry tears or drip oil. Or a ghostlike figure makes a sudden appearance, a disembodied spirit that frightens or confuses people. Often, after investigation, examiners discover that it is a hoax and manipulated by those seeking followers.

The Woman with Feathers and Blood

I will never forget the controversy during the 1980s over supernatural manifestations. A woman minister was speaking in charismatic churches and conferences in the United States. Her fame had grown quickly as a result of the supernatural manifestations associated with her. Often when she approached the platform to speak, bloody wounds had already appeared on her hands and feet. Drops of blood were sometimes visible on her forehead. When the back of her dress was opened, red streaks marked her back, ostensibly representative of the stripes on the back of Jesus.

Pastors were urged not to allow this woman to speak in their churches. They were warned that the manifestations they were seeing were not from God. But many pastors refused to heed the warning. When they were asked to give a Scripture to justify what was happening, they used this passage:

> "I will grant wonders in the sky above and signs on the earth below, blood, and fire, and vapor of smoke. The sun will be turned into darkness and the moon into blood, before the great and glorious day of the Lord shall come."
>
> Acts 2:19–20

No one could explain what this Scripture had to do with the woman's stigmata. But pastors argued that the woman had impressive character qualities. She loved Jesus, they said, and demonstrated the fruit of the Spirit in her life. The pastors also argued that leaders of large churches and ministries were endorsing her.

There was little understanding that character does not nullify the origin of manifestations, and that it does not matter who validates a person. A biblical foundation and the gift of discerning of spirits were still needed for what was happening. But despite pleading and reasoning, many of the pastors did not listen.

Some intercessors sought private counsel concerning the churches that had invited this woman to preach. Congregants were told not to speak a word against her. If they did, they were told they would be touching God's anointed: "Do not touch My anointed ones, and do My prophets no harm" (Psalm 105:15). They were also told that if anyone said anything negative against her, that person would come under a curse.

Inside their own spirits, the intercessors were in great turmoil. They were discerning spirits that were not from God. They feared that deception had invaded their congregations. In humility they sought prayer from others because they loved their pastors and churches.

One evening, during a meeting the woman was leading that happened to be videotaped, people in the congregation were told to close their eyes and worship Jesus. After a worship song, when they were told to open their eyes, the woman said that the Holy Spirit had flown over like a dove while they were worshiping and left a remnant of His presence—feathers! Sure enough, there they were.

It was not until some time after the meeting that the videotape was analyzed and slowed down to get a closer look. The woman had actually pulled feathers from her handkerchief, while most people's eyes had been closed, and dropped them around the platform.

Rick Renner, in his book *Merchandising the Anointing*, details the footage from the event:

> The video was put on slow motion to make sure every movement of the hand could be seen as feathers were dropped by this "prophetess" around the stage. It appeared that she was manipulating the feathers out of her handkerchief. This exhibition was no more than a magician's sleight of hand. At one point, you could actually see her passing feathers from one hand to the other as she prepared to drop them on the floor. There was no doubt that this was a fraud. *It was documented.*[1]

The discovery of fraud must have been devastating to those who believed in this woman. Although I had sensed something wrong from the first time I heard about the supernatural phenomena surrounding her ministry, only now did I know for certain that what I had sensed in my spirit was true.

What about the stigmata that this woman displayed? The question is not whether the blood or pain was real, but rather the source of it. There is much controversy surrounding stigmata, and we will discuss this issue in chapter 8.

By the way, this woman is still speaking and ministering today.

How Does Deception Take Place?

You may be like me and sense, at times, that something is wrong. Although you may not have the facts to prove it, do not accept a supernatural phenomenon merely because others are endorsing it. Wait until the Holy Spirit reveals the truth to you. This may take time. Be patient.

Lying signs may be supernatural in their origin. An example of this is firewalking—the practice of walking on hot coals, rocks or cinders without burning the feet. In some cultures, like India, it is part of a religious ritual. A current popular motivational speaker in the United States uses firewalking as an example of how people can overcome limited beliefs, phobias and fears. He believes that this kind of activity can turn fear into power.[2]

But these expressions of supernatural power influence people in the wrong way. And how do Christian leaders get taken in? How did the pastors get taken in by the woman with the bleeding hands and feathers? How does a person reach the place where he or she becomes unteachable?

One reason is the belief that the person in question is a special vessel of God. Others, they feel, are not quite as gifted and therefore unable to be used in such powerful manifestations of the Spirit.

These leaders seem to forget that Jesus promised His followers that "he who believes in Me, the works that I do, he will do also; and greater works than these he will do; because I go to the Father" (John 14:12). We can look into Scripture to discover the works of Jesus, and nowhere does Scripture limit this promise of Jesus to only those who are "extraordinarily gifted."

Another way a person reaches the place of being unteachable is when enthusiastic followers believe this person is different from the average believer. You are told you should not question the uniqueness of the *gift*. This minister is more "advanced" than others and lives on a higher spiritual level. The person should not be examined, therefore, by those who do not accept the manifestations.

We must be aware when someone comes with the appearance of a new supernatural manifestation. The Word of God has no substitution. Theologians who know how to use discernment must come to the forefront and help the Body of Christ receive *present* truth while not abandoning the Word of God in order to pursue "deeper" spirituality:

> Therefore, I will always be ready to remind you of these things, even though you already know them, and have been established in the truth which is present with you.
>
> 2 Peter 1:12

Neither of the first two events I mentioned happened instantly. The apparition of the virgin Mary had occurred for years. The woman with the bleeding hands and feathers ministered over a period of several years before her lying signs and wonders were uncovered.

Deception does not overtake a person instantly. A gradual process takes place when any person is drawn into deception. Jesus warned us to expect deceptive activities like this to happen. "False Christs and false prophets will arise and will show great signs and wonders, so as to mislead, if possible, even the elect" (Matthew 24:24). Evil spirits can entice believers and draw them into deception in several ways.

Counterfeit Presence of God

A counterfeit presence of God opens a person to various physical manifestations. The person slowly yields to these sensory manifestations, thinking that he or she is yielding to God. After a period of time, the person might feel sensations in the body like the agony associated with Jesus' crucifixion. The person might see this as "the fellowship of His sufferings" (Philippians 3:10). He or she might even experience the pain of death, such as nails being driven into the hands or feet. (The woman I mentioned earlier shared these experiences in her testimony.) At this point lying spirits can work any way they desire due to the level of deception that has occurred.

Counterfeit Guidance

Another way a person can be enticed into deception is through counterfeit guidance. A voice will compel the person to "Do this" or "Don't do that." There is no reason for the action and it can actually be contrary to the person's will. But the person continues to yield to the impulse and inner voice, looking for supernatural direction and guidance. He must have providential circumstances or direct guidance before taking action. At this point the person is vulnerable to deceiving spirits.

Joseph Smith, who wrote the Book of Mormon, is an example of this. Smith had several supernatural visitations. During these visitations he received direction and revelation. He followed the instruction of these voices of deception and eventually influenced millions of people with his false teachings.

The Lord gave us brains and a will. He does not expect us to get rid of either when we commit our lives to Jesus Christ. If we stop using our minds, our will and our other faculties, and if we turn aside from the foundation of God's Word, we open ourselves to deception.

Sometimes believers are told, "Get out of your mind!" But I would prefer to steer us back to Scripture, where Paul writes, "Be transformed by the renewing of your mind" (Romans 12:2) and "We have the mind of Christ" (1 Corinthians 2:16).

The apostle Peter had a powerful experience with the Lord on the Mount of Transfiguration. After that tremendous experience, he left us an admonition that "we have the prophetic word made more sure"

(2 Peter 1:19). It is clear that God's Word supported his experience. Rick Renner explains this Scripture in his book *Merchandising the Anointing*:

> Notice that Peter calls the Word of God "a more sure word of prophecy." This was a phrase used during his day to describe the writings of the Old Testament. They were called "the prophetical word." There is no doubt that this is a reference to the scriptures of the Old Testament. Peter tells us that they are "a more sure word."
>
> The phrase "more sure" is taken from the Greek word *bebaioteros* (be-bai-o-te-ros) and it refers to something that is "certain, stable or immovable." This is something which we would say is "set in concrete." It is the ultimate picture of stability and reliability.[3]

We can see that people who love God and are seeking a deeper walk with Him can be drawn into deception. Whenever we justify unusual manifestations as proof of spirituality, we are on shaky ground. Waiting for physical sensations as proof of the presence of God opens the door to deception. Listening for a voice before making simple decisions in life leaves a person vulnerable to deceiving spirits.

How we need a strong foundation in the Word of God to bring stability to our lives! The Scriptures give us a sure word that will keep us certain, stable and immovable in our walk with the Lord.

How to Discern Deception

We have seen so far that we need to use our minds but we also need to use the spiritual gift of discerning of spirits. So how do we discern when deception is operating?

Spiritual Sight

One way to discern is by seeing. The Lord sometimes opens our spiritual eyes and we can actually see the spirit. Visions occur when our spiritual eyes are open to the unseen realm.

Sometimes God opens our eyes to see beyond the physical world and peer into the unseen world. We may see not only the world of darkness but also the world of light:

> Then Elisha prayed and said, "O LORD, I pray, open his eyes that he may see." And the LORD opened the servant's eyes and he saw; and behold, the mountain was full of horses and chariots of fire all around Elisha.
>
> 2 Kings 6:17

Once Elisha's servant had his spiritual eyes opened, he was able to see more warring angels assisting them than the Aramean army against them.

Discerning a Wrong Spirit

Another way to discern spirits is to receive the name or nature of the spirit directly from God. When the gift of discerning of spirits is in operation, we do not need to ask the spirit its name. We are able to discern its identity by means of the supernatural gift given to us.

The apostle Paul discerned a spirit of divination in the girl in Philippi who kept following them and annoying them. He turned to the girl but addressed the spirit: "I command you in the name of Jesus Christ to come out of her!" (Acts 16:18). The spirit obeyed Paul and left the girl. Paul did not need to talk to the spirit. He simply discerned the spirit and took authority over it. You and I as believers are enabled, by the gift of God, to do the same thing.

Throughout the Bible we find examples of those who discerned a wrong spirit in someone who was both deceived and deceiving.

One of these deceivers was Simon the sorcerer (see Acts 8:9–24). He practiced magic and astonished the crowds in Samaria with his power. He participated in lying signs and wonders. People even said, "This man is what is called the Great Power of God" (verse 10). Although Simon was involved in occult activity, he listened to Philip's preaching, was convicted in his heart of sin and became a believer, even following through with baptism.

After becoming a Christian, Simon observed Peter and John as they laid hands on believers to receive the Holy Spirit. He had known the power of the occult but had never seen the power of God, and he recognized the power that these apostles possessed. I once heard a teacher say that Simon probably thought in his heart, *If I had this power, I could be an important man. Every man has a price.* So he offered Peter and John money in exchange for the gift they possessed.

Peter rebuked him:

> "May your silver perish with you, because you thought you could obtain the gift of God with money! You have no part or portion in this matter, for your heart is not right before God. Therefore repent of this wickedness of yours, and pray the Lord that, if possible, the intention of your heart may be forgiven you. For I see that you are in the gall of bitterness and in the bondage of iniquity."
>
> Acts 8:20–23

Peter had seen something that his physical eyes could not see. He discerned a wrong spirit operating through Simon. Peter was also indignant at the prospect of a believer merchandising the works of God.

It is evident that a born-again experience, as Simon apparently had, does not guarantee that the heart has been cleansed from evil. Believers can be deceived by their own hearts, and mature believers are needed to help us see the areas of our hearts that still need to be purified.

Sanctification is a process and takes place over a period of time. And discipleship in the Body of Christ is essential for new believers to mature in the Word of God and in character.

Let's look at two more examples of first-century apostles discerning a wrong spirit.

The deceived man in the first story was a Jewish false prophet (see Acts 13:6–12). Paul and Barnabas had been invited to share the Word of God with the proconsul Sergius Paulus. But the false prophet, a magician named Elymas, opposed them and tried to turn the proconsul away from faith. Paul, discerning evil spirits operating through Elymas, exclaimed, "You who are full of all deceit and fraud, you son of the devil, you enemy of all righteousness, will you not cease to make crooked the straight ways of the Lord?" (verse 10). When Elymas was temporarily blinded, the proconsul, observing the power of God in Paul, put his faith in the Lord Jesus Christ.

The power of God through discerning of spirits will catch the attention of unbelievers. This gift can be an evangelistic tool to bring unbelievers into the Kingdom of God.

One final example of discerning of spirits is found in the story of Ananias and Sapphira (see Acts 5:1–11).

Some of the believers must have become popular when they sold their property and gave the money to the church. This husband and wife must also have wanted the approval of their fellow believers. So they sold some property and came to the assembly with money, secretly keeping some of the proceeds for themselves. After telling Peter that they were bringing all the money from the sale of their property, the apostle asked, "Why has Satan filled your heart to lie to the Holy Spirit and to keep back some of the price of the land?" (verse 3). Ananias and Sapphira fell dead within minutes of each other. This demonstration of the power of God brought holy fear on the entire body of believers.

The Church today also needs to learn to walk in a holy fear of God. Not fear in the sense of terror, but an awesome respect for God and His righteousness. Displays of the discerning of spirits and the power of God will help to bring this about.

Discernment is not some cute spiritual game, though some see it that way. It can bring tremendous inspiration and strength to the Church. This gift helps to protect against false doctrines, lying signs and wonders, apparitions, lies and all that is counterfeit. It helps leaders choose the proper men and women for positions in ministry. May the Lord open our spiritual eyes and activate the gift of discerning of spirits in the Body of Christ.

In the next chapter we will take a look at seducing spirits and doctrines of demons. How thankful I am for the power of the Holy Spirit. Only His power can keep us free from the power of deception!

Prayer

Father, I ask You to help me be aware of every deceptive trap of the enemy. Let the Scriptures light my path and keep me from the dark deception of the enemy. Open my eyes not only to see wrong spirits but to see truth. I ask You to activate the gift of discerning of spirits in my life. Thank You, Lord, for empowering me with Your Holy Spirit to walk free from deception. In Jesus' name, Amen.

For Further Reflection

1. Have you ever known a person caught in deception? What happened?
2. Describe the dangers of providential guidance and the path to deception.
3. Describe a time when your spiritual eyes were opened to see into the unseen world.
4. How can Christians have evil powers working through them?
5. List some ways that discerning of spirits can help bring inspiration and security to the Church.

4

Seducing Spirits and Doctrines of Demons

Emotions were running high. People felt confused and many were angry. Word had finally reached the media concerning some wild stories about a controversial independent church in the northwestern United States. It seemed impossible that a 3,500-member congregation had allowed and even encouraged some of the things that were happening. Families leaving the church wondered how they ever had become entrapped in its teaching and practices. Two of the controversial developments were seductive dances in the church and the murder of a child by her mother.

The 37-year-old woman, convinced that killing her five-year-old was the only way to save her, had drowned the little girl in a motel bathtub. If the child grew up, the mother believed, she would risk a life of demonic possession and eternal damnation. Dying before she reached the age of reason would guarantee her life in heaven.

The mother, accused of murder, was later committed to a psychiatric hospital. She had been unstable, but critics of the church felt she had become preoccupied with demons. They also felt the preoccupation was the result of teachings from the pastor of the church.

Many observers felt this church had begun emphasizing demons after the pastor was criticized by a group of dissidents. Suicides and broken marriages in the congregation had been blamed not only on the unconventional teachings but on a preoccupation with demons.

One of the controversial teachings by the pastor was a series of lectures on "spiritual and soulical relationships." He decreed that the highest form of spiritual realization could be found by dancing at church services with someone else's spouse. Dancing with your "spiritual connection," said the pastor, could open up the possibility of pure spiritual love.

The teachings from this pastor allowed "connected" couples to express the love of Jesus and the unity of the church by putting their spirits together. They were encouraged to hold hands, hug, embrace and even kiss each other. These expressions were deemed proper forms of spiritual expression as long as the motivation was pure.

The pastor distinguished between "soulical" connections, the connection between husband and wife, and "spiritual" connections, an experience of Christ realized in a loving dance with someone other than your spouse. The pastor did forewarn that the soulical and spiritual could get confused, so he admonished the dancing connections not to hold each other too long, stare too intensely or waltz. He told men who would become sexually aroused during this time just to keep on dancing. Special rooms were designated for dancing, as well as dancing in the hallways and pews.[1]

Some observers felt that part of the crisis of the mother who had drowned her daughter had been a painful, unorthodox experience with her male "connection." He had fallen in love with her, but she felt the relationship was wrong. Since she did not know how to reconcile her feelings, and since those in the church simply tried to cast out her demons, she suffered a mental breakdown.

Years later, after the pastor was accused of sexual assault during counseling sessions, he was dismissed, ordered to turn in his keys and leave the church. He was also sued by a victimized paraplegic and for sexual advances of adults toward children.[2]

Seducing Spirits

This case may sound bizarre, but wrong teachings can infiltrate even churches that have been established in sound doctrine. The apostle Paul gave Timothy, his son in the faith, a strong caution that every Christian of every era must heed: "The Spirit explicitly says that in later times some will fall away from the faith, paying attention to deceitful spirits and doctrines of demons" (1 Timothy 4:1).

Men were coming to Ephesus with strange revelations and advocating odd, supernatural activities that endangered believers. The fundamentals of the faith were in jeopardy of being twisted and perverted. Paul realized that deceitful spirits—what the King James Version calls "seducing spirits"—were behind these teachings, creeping into churches, operating through false prophets and false teachers and causing great spiritual error. Believers were being led away from the truth, seduced by evil spirits.

There are churches today that teach a form of prayer according to a strange revelation. This form of prayer encourages the person to empty the mind of thought by repeating a word or phrase or even focusing on one's breath. In this form of prayer there needs to be a complete lack of thought—any thought. The purpose is to cause the person to enter an altered state of consciousness in order to find one's true self. By doing this, they believe, they will find God.

The Bible never tells us to empty our minds. Our minds are to be transformed. Jesus also admonished His followers, "You shall

LOVE THE LORD YOUR GOD WITH ALL YOUR HEART, AND WITH ALL YOUR SOUL, AND WITH *ALL YOUR MIND*" (Matthew 22:37, emphasis added).

How do the kinds of evil, seducing spirits that deliver such deception infiltrate the Church?

False Teachers and Prophets

Some error comes invariably from false teachers. They weave Scriptures together skillfully by taking them out of context; by picking them over a wide field and putting them together; or by other means of changing the meaning of God's Word. Paul, by contrast, wrote, "We do not use deception, nor do we distort the word of God" (2 Corinthians 4:2, NIV).

False teachers may also use supernatural signs and wonders as a means of monetary gain. Their stories and claims can be untrue or tremendously exaggerated. But believers who do not accept these claims may be accused of a lack of faith or going on a witch hunt.

False teachers refuse to accept correction when confronted with truth. They may become angry and pour ridicule, slander or hatred on the one who brings correction or questions the doctrine.

A false prophet is a person who illegitimately claims charismatic authority within religious circles. This individual uses the gift for evil purposes. The person can use "prophecy" to control certain individuals or even to gain monetary profit from them. A prophet can be labeled *false* by one group and *true* by another.

In recent days a well-known leader was removed from ministry due to immorality. A team of his own choosing was assigned to help restore him. Yet the minister refused the restoration process and left town with his girlfriend. He refused to accept correction from the very leaders who wanted his life and ministry to be restored.

False prophets are dangerous. Often people will follow the "words" they release without questioning them.

I remember a minister years ago who prophesied that everyone in the meeting who gave a thousand dollars could be sure that a surgeon's scalpel would never touch their bodies. Checkbooks came out from purses and pockets. People borrowed money. They wanted the promise of health and were willing to do whatever it took to donate the money to this false prophet.

Deceived Teachers

Some error also comes from deceived teachers. They may not be misleading believers intentionally but are themselves deceived by accepting and commending everything supernatural as coming from God. Supernatural signs, as we have seen, are no proof that a ministry or teacher has revelation from God.

The seducing spirits Paul warned against in 1 Timothy 4:1 attempt to mingle error with truth for those responsible for teaching doctrine. Every believer must, therefore, test what is being taught against the Word of God. Christians must also check the teacher's attitude toward the authority of Scripture, the atoning cross of Christ and other fundamental truths of the Gospel.

The character of the teacher is not a reliable means of testing the teacher's doctrine, since good teachers can be deceived and since a life full of good works is not evidence of God's endorsement. Satan's ministers "disguise themselves as servants of righteousness" (2 Corinthians 11:15).

"The Great Pretender" was a popular song many years ago. Just like the song says, these false teachers are great pretenders who "pretend too much." They may be sincere but are trying to force themselves into a gift or position that God did not intend for them to have. They see what God is doing and want to be part of the latest thing in the Body of Christ. As they attempt to function in places where God did not put them, they present "new revelations" to wow the spiritually naïve or ignorant. Often they purport that others are not mature enough to receive their fresh revelation.

The goal of seducing spirits: to bring teaching that originates from the pit of hell. This is what Paul called "doctrines of demons."

Doctrines of Demons

Many denominations and churches believe in the doctrine of demons. Let's look again at what Paul taught: "The Spirit explicitly says that in later times some will fall away from the faith, paying attention to deceitful spirits and doctrines of demons" (1 Timothy 4:1).

"Doctrines of demons" consists of ideas that a person believes, but which are actually the result of suggestions made to his mind by deceiving spirits. The simplest definition of *doctrines of demons*, therefore, is "doctrines created by demons."

Someone who accepts these teachings as truth probably believes they originated from God since they were received as a supernatural "download." Doctrines of demons are the fruit of a mind that has been seduced by wrong teaching and information. That mind or conscience has become dull and insensitive.

A person's spirit must be awake and sensitized to the evil spirits seducing him or her with a strange doctrine. Otherwise that person will accept the teaching as true rather than rebuke the evil spirit attempting to steer him or her off course.

The deceived person will first listen to the spirits—again, probably thinking he is listening to God. Then he will obey the spirits. And ultimately he will pass along their "new revelation." These teachings may include lies about sin, holiness, God's presence, His love or many other spiritual-sounding ideas.

The very first example of a doctrine of demons is found in Genesis, when the serpent twisted the word of God to the woman. Contradicting what God had said concerning eating the fruit of the tree in the middle of the Garden, the serpent told her, "You surely will not die!" (Genesis 3:4). When the woman listened and obeyed the new doctrine, she fell into deception.

Doctrines of demons are foundations for all the major religions, with the exception of Christianity. Muhammad, for example, is the central figure of Islam and regarded by Muslims as the latest and greatest of the prophets of God. At age forty he started receiving revelations from a source he thought was God and proclaiming that "God is one." Muhammad and his followers migrated to Medina (now in Saudi Arabia) in the year A.D. 622. This marks the beginning of the Islamic calendar. The revelations (or *Ayat*—meaning "signs of God") that Muhammad received until his death in A.D. 632 form the verses of the Quran, the "word of God." These teachings are the basis of Islam, which now has between one and two billion adherents, according to differing statistics from various resources, and is second in size only to Christianity.[3]

Any teaching must be tested against the revealed Word of God. Truth is always in harmony with the Bible. Doctrines that originate from demonic spirits undermine God's Word.

Discounting Scripture's Authority

One of the ways Scripture is undermined is by discounting its authority. Many churches today teach that there is error in the Bible. But if this were true, however small the error, there would be no guarantee that the rest of the Bible is true.

> All Scripture is inspired by God and profitable for teaching, for reproof, for correction, for training in righteousness; so that the man of God may be adequate, equipped for every good work.
>
> 2 Timothy 3:16–17

Some who follow biblical principles, including denominational leaders, dismiss the miracles of Jesus. They deny that Jesus took human sin on Himself when He died on the cross. And they deny that He actually rose from the dead. They say, moreover, that these things do not much matter one way or the other. But the Bible teaches that "He made Him who knew no sin to be sin on our behalf" (2 Corinthians

61

5:21) and that "if Christ has not been raised, then our preaching is vain, [and] your faith also is vain" (1 Corinthians 15:14).

Scripture is undermined by the teaching that Christians should not hold only with the Bible, but incorporate understanding from other religions and traditions as well. This "inclusive" approach may accept recently discovered heretical manuscripts such as the Gnostic Gospel of Judas, as well as holy books from other religions, and chants or ceremonies from non-Christian faiths that actually contradict Scripture.

Distorting Scripture's Teachings

Another way Scripture can be undermined is by distorting its teachings. Some false religions accept Jesus Christ as the Son of God, but they do not believe He is divine or coequal with God. They acknowledge Him merely as a prophet.

Christadelphians are one group that distorts the Bible. They believe God is the Creator of all things, the Father of true believers, and that He is a separate being from His Son, Jesus Christ. The Holy Spirit, they believe, is the power of God used in creation and for salvation. Christadelphians reject the idea that Christ could die as a replacement sacrifice for mankind. They do not believe His one-time sacrifice can cover sins forever. Sins can be forgiven, they believe, only if we walk the path of self-denial. They also teach that after death believers are in a state of self-existence until the resurrection at the return of Jesus Christ.[4]

Jehovah's Witnesses also distort Scripture by denying the deity of Jesus. Here is a favorite verse of the Jehovah's Witnesses:

> "You heard that I said to you, 'I go away, and I will come to you.' If you loved Me, you would have rejoiced because I go to the Father, for the Father is greater than I."
>
> John 14:28

The term *greater* in this verse refers to the Father's position rather than to His nature. Jesus and the Father are one. But Jehovah's Witnesses use this passage to contradict the Nicene and Apostles' creeds, which state that the three Persons of the Trinity are coequal and coeternal.

In the next major section, I will describe an example I have found in Asia of a distortion of Scripture that leads to serious deception.

Adding Human Thoughts

A third way demonic spirits undermine the Scriptures is by adding human thoughts. Some segments of the Body of Christ teach that our thoughts can actually become the thoughts of God. But the Bible states that " 'My thoughts are not your thoughts, nor are your ways My ways,' declares the LORD" (Isaiah 55:8).

Certain groups, some going back many hundreds of years, have taught that we can reach sinless perfection during our lifetimes on earth. The Holiness movement, starting in the early nineteenth century, taught that, after conversion, one could be freed from sin and the character flaws that cause sin. This doctrine is referred to in Holiness churches as "entire sanctification," though it used to be called Christian perfection.[5]

One of the most extensive attempts at sinlessness is found in monasticism. Gregory of Nyssa, one of the greatest Eastern leaders in the struggle for perfection, saw Jesus as the prototype of the Christian life that can be lived in sinless perfection.

The second-century Montanists taught that men could become gods.[6]

During the twelfth through the fourteenth centuries, the Albigensians said that the human spirit is capable of freeing itself from the flesh in order to become one with God.[7]

The late medieval period saw the Brethren of the Free Spirit, who believed that man could advance in perfection beyond God.[8]

The English Ranters in the seventeenth century saw it as logically impossible for "perfected man" to sin.[9] And the nineteenth-century Oneida community looked for ways to reconcile sinlessness with the impure desires of the flesh.[10] The idea of sinless perfection has been a trap of the enemy that causes mankind to attempt to live a perfect life. The idea that achieving perfection will bring us closer to God is a deception that distorts good works.

Each of these groups added their own deceptive thoughts to the teachings of Scripture. These doctrines are designed to lead believers away from truth and into deception.

Putting Scripture Aside

A final way that Scripture can be undermined is by putting it aside entirely and replacing it with human ideas and self-improvement methods.

Many major television personalities promote a religion of self-help. Millions of viewers are now embracing innovative spiritual beliefs that attempt to make man his own god.

Influential celebrities promote a church-free spirituality to their audiences. Their influence on culture is far greater than that of university presidents, politicians, even religious leaders. A generic spirituality has normalized philosophies that perceive all religions as equally valid paths to God.

Often the concepts come from a variety of unconventional Western and Eastern religions, including spiritual psychotherapy, Christ-consciousness, New Age philosophies, karmic destiny (Zen Buddhism), reincarnation (Hinduism) and a long list of other spiritual self-help schemes. Through international talk shows, billions of dollars, bestselling books, philanthropic works and controversial self-help methods, a media counterculture has been established, and the faddish, misleading self-help programs promote a quick-fix material culture. This type of influence, when belief systems are not established on truths found in the Word of God, is deceptive—and can be highly appealing.

How sad that in their hunger for the supernatural, even believers will abandon all reason, sound doctrine and common sense in falling for these deceptions!

Ancestor Worship

Here is an example of a way Scripture can be undermined through distortion.

The Bible gives commands concerning honor and obedience to our parents: "Honor your father and your mother, that your days may be prolonged in the land which the LORD your God gives you" (Exodus 20:12) and "Children, obey your parents in the Lord, for this is right" (Ephesians 6:1).

There are groups, however, that distort these Scriptures. I first noticed this distortion when I began to travel to Asia. Although some of the people I was ministering to were Christians, they continued to cling to old customs involving ancestor worship. Even adult children with their own grandchildren harbored great concern about obeying parents. This, I was told, was their culture. But over time I realized that some of it was rooted in ancestor worship.

Some Asian believers claim that ancestor worship should really be termed *veneration*. They do not worship parents as deity, they say, but simply become better persons through fulfilling their duty as offspring. One reporter I read says the practice comes from Confucius and Laozi rather than from religion.

Nevertheless, a definition of ancestral worship usually includes the belief not only that these deceased ancestors continue to exist, but that they are interested in the affairs of the world and are able to influence the lives, including the finances, of those who are still living. Some of the practices associated with ancestor worship (or veneration): visiting graves; leaving offerings of food or other practical items (such as toothbrushes); communicating with dead ancestors; and setting up candles and "sugar skulls" to revere the deceased.

Some Asians regard ancestors as guardian angels who provide protection. Some cults believe they can redeem their dead ancestors. Others say their dead ancestors can actually become minor deities.

Ancestor worship practices continue in some cultures even after the adult child becomes a Christian.[11]

The Lord asks us to honor our parents, and He asks children to obey parents. But adults are not children. Parents can advise their adult children but must give them the liberty to live their own lives. Distorting the teaching of God's Word causes people to come under a spirit of control, thinking they must continue to obey the parent's wishes after they become adults. (We will see an example of this in chapter 10.)

But we need to understand the whole Bible! Otherwise we can be led astray by a distortion of Scripture.

Contending Earnestly

The New Testament Church was made aware of the deception by seducing spirits sent to lure believers away from the faith. Jude admonished his readers about the evil attempting to invade the Church. He declared outright war on the false teachers and false prophets who had crept in unnoticed to cause division and who were abusing God's people.

Jude did not distinguish between those who were outright liars, those who were deceived and those who were spiritually ignorant. Whatever the reason for misleading the people, Jude confronted the issues at hand.

I am sure he recognized that some of those false teachers had been pure at one time. He was not judging their hearts. He was simply dealing with issues and the fruit of their ministries. So it was that Jude exhorted believers to "contend"[12]:

> While I was making every effort to write you about our common salvation, I felt the necessity to write to you appealing that you *contend earnestly for the faith* which was once for all handed down to the saints.
>
> Jude 3, emphasis added

The believers were in a battle, and this was no time to wear blindfolds. The conflict was not about personality, style or excuses (if the ministers in question, for example, had a painful background). No, the faith of believers was in danger of being subverted, so this was simply a time for believers to take responsibility, to hold fast to the truth.

One of the areas in which we need to hold fast is evaluating some of the teaching current leaders are passing along from trips to heaven. My recommendation: *Be careful with revelation from these trips. Recognize that extrabiblical revelation cannot be proved or disproved. It is always safe, however, when we check it against God's Word.*[13]

I remember many popular speakers talking about trips to heaven during the peak of the charismatic renewal in the 1960s and '70s. Their testimonies kept audiences spellbound and their books became bestsellers. The trips to heaven were not the real issue. The issue was the "revelation" they received in heaven and the assignments to go back to earth and teach what they had heard. I am not saying that all trips to heaven and all messages from these trips were wrong. I am simply saying that we need to judge all teaching against the Word of God and by the Spirit of God.

The Bible gives some information about heaven. It does not tell us everything. Yet many of the teachers today, when describing their visits to heaven, also discuss their conversations with people who have died and are waiting there.

Biblical characters who visited or experienced heaven (perhaps in the spirit) were filled with adoration and awe at having seen the Lord. Their experience was described only as one of worship and great joy in the presence of God.

The apostle Paul made a visit to heaven. When he wrote of his experience, he said he had heard "unspeakable words, which it is not lawful for a man to utter" (2 Corinthians 12:4, KJV). If Paul was not able to share what he heard, does it not stand to reason that we need to be careful in speaking new revelation without the proper checks and balances in place?

One of these checks and balances, as we have seen earlier, is a strong foundation in the Word of God. Many reports from current leaders reveal that most Christians today do not know even the very basics of the Bible.

Another check is the operation of the Holy Spirit's guidance. He will alert you when a wrong spirit is in operation. Do not ignore the Spirit's warning.

A third check is making sure you are connected to a pastor or leader who can help you discern. Mature spiritual leaders are able to guide believers into truth. Be sure you are in proper alignment with those who are grounded in God's Word and who have a good reputation in spiritual matters.

Those who visit heaven today may be truthful in sharing their experiences. We simply cannot validate them by the Word of God.

"Let Me Lead You"

In 1965, knowing that the Church today would be facing infiltration of seducing spirits and doctrines of demons, the Lord gave a prophetic vision of coming deception to Stanley Frodsham, the author of *Smith Wigglesworth: Apostle of Faith*. Frodsham prophesied:

> When one shall turn to the right hand or to the left, you shall not turn with them, but keep your eyes wholly on the Lord. The coming days are the most dangerous, difficult and dark, but there shall be a mighty outpouring of My Spirit upon many cities; and many shall be destroyed. My people must be diligently warned concerning the days that are ahead. Many shall turn after seducing spirits; many are already seducing My people. It is those who do righteousness that are righteous. Many cover their sins by great theological words. But I warn you of seducing spirits who instruct My people in an evil way.
>
> Many shall come with seducing spirits and hold out lustful enticements. You will find that after I have visited My people again, the way shall become more and more narrow, and fewer shall walk therein. But

be not deceived, the ways of righteousness are My ways. For though Satan comes as an angel of light (2 Corinthians 11:13–15), hearken not to him; for those who perform miracles and speak not righteousness are not of Me. I warn you with great intensity that I am going to judge My house and have a church without spot or wrinkle when I come. I desire to open your eyes and give you spiritual understanding, that you may not be deceived, but may walk in uprightness of heart before Me, loving righteousness and hating every evil way. Look unto Me, and I will make you to perceive with the eyes of the Spirit the things that lurk in darkness that are not visible to the human eye. Let Me lead you in this way that you may perceive the powers of darkness and battle against them. It is not a battle against flesh and blood, for if you battle in that way, you accomplish nothing. But if you let Me take over and battle against the powers of darkness, then they are defeated; and then liberation is brought to My people.[14]

Although this prophetic word (which can be read in the appendix on page 170) was released many years ago, it is a message we need now. God desires to raise up a mature Church that will, in the words of Jude, contend earnestly for the faith, so that believers are protected from the snares of the evil one.

A great weapon of protection for believers is the ability to judge the supernatural. The next chapter will help us better understand this weapon so we can guard against the deception intended to hinder God's people.

Prayer

Heavenly Father, I ask You to help me discern any false or deceived teachers and prophets. Help me be able to recognize the true ones. Let Your Word come alive in my spirit so that I can also discern doctrines of demons. Help me to be drawn to You and not to seducing spirits that seek to draw me away from Your true presence and from Your Word. I want to love righteousness and hate evil. With Your help, I will follow after

You and resist every wrong and deceptive spirit. Thank You for opening the eyes of my spirit so that I can walk free from deception. In Jesus' name, Amen.

For Further Reflection

1. Think about the difference between false teachers and deceived teachers.
2. Why is character not a test for the validity of a particular teaching?
3. What are doctrines of demons?
4. How does a seducing spirit operate?
5. What are some of the ways teachings can be twisted to bring about deception?

5

Judging the Supernatural

The atmosphere was electric! People started arriving an hour before the scheduled time. By the time the event began, 1,500 students and parents packed the stadium. The top ten senior girls from the drill team would be picked that evening to be the drill team officers. Out of the ten, only one would be selected captain. The drill team captain held a higher honor at this school than the homecoming queen!

Our daughter, Lori, was in the tryouts. Judges were brought in from various states to judge the dance routines. Each girl was to choreograph her own routine without any outside help. The judges were assigned to assess originality, talent, expertise and other aspects of the dance. The judges, experts in their fields, used their professional skills to evaluate each girl by a specific set of standards. Their judgment would determine the outcome.

At the end of the evening the announcement was made. Lori was selected not only as one of the officers but also as captain of the drill team. What a thrilling time for our family!

Judges are used not just for school functions but also in many areas of life and society. They form the backbone of our judicial system. Judges are high-ranking court officers who supervise court trials, instruct juries and pronounce sentences. A good judge is highly respected in society. A bad judge, on the other hand, is a stench in our nostrils. Many times bad judges are removed from their positions when they fail to uphold their responsibility to judge well.

We accept the role of judges in society even though often we do not accept the role of judging in church life. Many believers are taught that Jesus' admonition "Do not judge so that you will not be judged" (Matthew 7:1) means that if they judge anything, they are in disobedience to God or could come under a curse. These believers may feel uneasy about a situation or person, but since they have been taught not to judge, they push down their uneasy feelings and try to accept what they see happening, regardless of what they sense about it.

This is not what Jesus was teaching. When He warned His listeners not to judge, He meant not judging by a single act or not judging the hearts of others, since only the Lord knows the heart. We may counsel a person but must never judge in an unloving way or in a spirit of revenge or by speaking evil of the person.

But even though we are told not to judge a person in these ways, that does not mean we are not to judge anything! Let's look at some of the ways we are instructed to judge.

What Do Christians Judge?

Paul told the church at Corinth, "Do you not know that we will judge *angels*?" (1 Corinthians 6:3, emphasis added). Since we have that assignment promised by the Lord for the Day of Judgment, He is preparing us now to be able to fulfill it.

Another area where believers are told to judge is *prophecy*: "Let two or three prophets speak, and let the others pass judgment" (1 Corinthians 14:29). All prophecy should be judged according to specific guidelines to ensure that the prophecy is from the Lord. One of the guidelines given: to judge the prophecy by Scripture.

True prophecy agrees with the letter and the spirit of Scripture. The Holy Spirit never contradicts Himself. He will not tell us in the Scriptures not to commit adultery, for example, and then tell us we are okay committing adultery if we really love the person. "All Scripture is inspired by God and profitable for teaching, for reproof, for correction, for training in righteousness" (2 Timothy 3:16). The Scriptures are to be used to reprove or judge a prophetic word that does not agree with either the letter or the spirit of God's Word. The Greek word for *reproof* comes from the word *elegchos*, which means "evidence or proof." The synonym of that word means "judgment."[1] So when you judge a prophetic message using Scripture, you are giving evidence from the Bible that the word is correct or not correct.

All prophetic messages must be in line with the written Word of God. They must be proven by the Scriptures to see if they are valid. In order for believers to be able to judge prophecy, therefore, they must know the Bible.

We are also told that mature spiritual people have the ability to judge *everything*! "He who is spiritual appraises all things, yet he himself is appraised by no one" (1 Corinthians 2:15). The person this passage is talking about has grown in his or her walk with the Lord. His or her senses have been sharpened to discern what is from God and what is not from God. "Solid food is for the mature, who because of practice have their senses trained to discern good and evil" (Hebrews 5:14).

Again the Bible admonishes believers to test *all things* and hold onto what is good: "Do not quench the Spirit; do not despise prophetic utterances. But examine everything carefully; hold fast to that which is good" (1 Thessalonians 5:19–21). We are not to accept all preaching, all prophetic messages or all supernatural happenings as truth.

We are also exhorted not to believe every spirit but to "test the spirits to see whether they are from God" (1 John 4:1). All revelation, prophecy and supernatural happenings must be tested or judged against God's Word, and also by the discerning of spirits.

How does this work?

Let Your Spirit Rule

Mankind is a three-part being: "Now may the God of peace Himself sanctify you entirely; and may your *spirit and soul and body* be preserved complete, without blame at the coming of our Lord Jesus Christ" (1 Thessalonians 5:23, emphasis added).

When God created the first human, He "formed man of dust from the ground, and breathed into his nostrils the breath of life; and man became a living being" (Genesis 2:7). When the Lord did this, He breathed *spirit* into Adam's *body*, which had been formed of clay. His body could relate to the external physical world through its senses of hearing, seeing, feeling, tasting and smelling. And man became a living being with a *soul*, meaning he now had a mind, will and emotions.

But it is through the spirit, as we have seen, that men and women are able to relate to God, who is the origin of life. Humans can hear from God by His Spirit. The soul and body, when rightly aligned, fall under the jurisdiction of the spirit. Otherwise individuals will be either "soulish"—that is, ruled by thoughts and feelings from the soul (mind, will and emotions)—or else "carnal," driven by the needs of the body. Men and women can either influence the world they live in by following the guidance God gives through His Spirit, or they can be influenced by the world by putting their own needs first.

Those who have spirits that are alive in Christ are able to discern and test spirits. But the Holy Spirit is able to work through the regenerated human spirit, and through the faculties of the soul and body, only when the will of the believer is engaged. In other words, the person has a choice! The person discerns in his spirit or simply knows—through the teaching of Scripture, for instance—what he needs to do. His will chooses to do it. And then his spirit enables him to fulfill the thought of his mind and the choice of his will.

Judging Rightly

When God brought together spirit and body in Adam, man became a living being with a soul. Adam possessed unthinkable power. He had tremendous knowledge and potential. He named every one of the animals. He had everything required to fulfill God's purposes on the earth. But, as Watchman Nee pointed out in his book *The Latent Power of the Soul,* the power that resided in Adam was locked up after the Fall.

The potential God put in man at the very beginning is still there. But ever since the Fall, this power has not been fully released. The work of the enemy is to stir up the soul of man and allow deceptive spiritual power to be released on the earth.

Many religions try to release this deceptive power. Instruction is given in Buddhism, Taoism, Hinduism and other religions to overcome the hindrances of the flesh and to give greater expression and release to this hidden power. Religions use various forms of ascetic practices, breathing exercises, simple forms of meditation, or others, all with the purpose of subjugating the body under the power of the soul so that the immobilized power within can be released. These adherents are then able to perform miracles of healing, even to predict the future.[2]

If we do not understand the principle behind some of these supernatural occurrences, we may be deceived by the release of the power of the soul.

When the mind is renewed by the Scriptures, however, and the emotions are in line with the heart of God, the person is able to discern what the Spirit is saying and then make decisions that are in line with God's will.

The spirit of man, in other words, can guide the soul, which tests the word it receives. "The one who joins himself to the Lord is one spirit with Him" (1 Corinthians 6:17). He is able to enter the presence of God through yielding his spirit, soul and body in worship.

In God's presence men and women are able to hear the Father and to know His verdict.

When we are judging supernatural phenomena, therefore, our spirits must be in tune with God's Holy Spirit. We can discern the source of what is happening. Our minds can then make a decision either to accept or to reject the supernatural as being from God or from the enemy.

Judging Wrongly

When a person's spirit, soul and body are not rightly aligned, he opens himself to deception in several ways. He may cease to use his mind to test what he is sensing in his spirit. When he depends solely on voices or impulses for direction in the details of life, he opens himself to guidance from evil spirits disguising themselves as God. He may wait for a confirming Scripture, circumstance or some other corroboration, and then he follows that voice without question.

A person may also operate too much in the soulish realm and wait for certain feelings. In this case he is yielding more and more to outside circumstances rather than to the voice of God in his spirit.

> You have an anointing from the Holy One, and all of you know the truth. I do not write to you because you do not know the truth, but because you do know it and because no lie comes from the truth.
>
> 1 John 2:20–21, NIV

Too often I have witnessed people in church services who prophesy because a certain *feeling* comes over them. Sometimes excitement and anticipation are in the atmosphere from a powerful worship service, a testimony or a sermon. The person's soul has been stirred, and he or she prophesies out of the emotion of the moment.

It also seems that when the soul is not stirred by external stimuli, the person is not exercising the gift of prophecy. But those feelings can deceive a person and cause him or her to operate out of the soulish realm rather than from the spirit, to which God's Spirit speaks.

Discerning Spirits

The Holy Spirit empowers the believer with the gift of discerning of spirits. This is no mental exercise. Rather, it is a supernatural gift given in the very moment it is needed. If the only ways to have spiritual discernment were to ponder with our minds and do research and pore over theological texts until we reached a conclusion, we would be in trouble! Only the highly educated would be able to discern and judge spirits, while the uneducated would be vulnerable to deception from evil spirits.

But God has given every believer the Holy Spirit. He promises to teach us all things and help us discern the source of any demonstration of the supernatural. The discerning of spirits is possible when a person is filled with the Holy Spirit.

An unbeliever cannot exercise this gift. "A natural man does not accept the things of the Spirit of God, for they are foolishness to him; and he cannot understand them, because they are spiritually appraised" (1 Corinthians 2:14). God's Spirit is given to believers as a weapon to free them from wrong spirits. When this gift is operating, a believer can know immediately what is motivating a person or situation.

A Quiet Nudge

At times the believer senses a nudging inside as to the source of a particular phenomenon. The Holy Spirit will alert the spirit of the believer and warn him or her, if necessary.

A friend sensed danger recently when her husband decided to enclose their porch. Although he had done many construction jobs in the past, that day she felt uneasy in her inner being and was not able to shake it. But her husband insisted he knew what he was doing and that there was no reason for concern.

About halfway through the job, he fell from the scaffolding and crushed the lower part of one leg. As he lay there with shattered bones and in great pain, he remembered the caution from his wife. The Holy Spirit had been giving her a warning. Good hindsight! From that point on, he decided to listen to his wife when she felt something was wrong!

A "Police Gift"

The discerning of spirits is given as a "police gift" to keep the enemy's influence from causing serious problems in the Body of Christ. Here are just two biblical examples of people who discerned an operation from the enemy.

First, when Gehazi, the servant of Elisha, pursued Naaman, the Aramean commander who had just been healed of leprosy, he asked for money and clothing for a fabricated cause—really just to enrich himself. When Gehazi returned and Elisha asked him where he had been, Gehazi replied that he had not been anywhere. Elisha, however, was able to discern the truth, and said,

> "Did not my heart go with you, when the man turned from his chariot to meet you? Is it a time to receive money and to receive clothes and olive groves and vineyards and sheep and oxen and male and female servants?"
>
> 2 Kings 5:26

Elisha discerned Gehazi's greed and deviousness, in spite of the servant's word to the contrary, and judged him accordingly.

Jesus discerned evil spirits and the activity of God's Spirit operating through people. When He asked Simon Peter who people thought He was, Peter concluded for himself that "You are the Christ, the Son of the living God" (Matthew 16:16). Jesus replied,

78

"Flesh and blood did not reveal this to you, but My Father who is in heaven" (verse 17). Yet a short time later this same Peter tried to talk Jesus out of His coming persecution and death. Jesus discerned a wrong spirit operating through Peter.

> He turned and said to Peter, "Get behind Me, Satan! You are a stumbling block to Me; for you are not setting your mind on God's interests, but man's."
>
> Matthew 16:23

When our spirits are awake and sensitive to the Holy Spirit, we are able to discern and test supernatural occurrences. Believers must not abandon reason and sound doctrine merely because they are spiritually hungry and desire a fresh move of the Spirit. Genuine miracles can be examined and tested.

Testing Miracles

Our youngest son, Mark, was miraculously healed when he was two years old. He had a condition that the doctors said would become cancerous by the time he was twenty. The required x-rays and physical exam confirmed the condition. Mark was anointed with oil and prayers were continually offered up to heaven. Two weeks later he was taken to surgery. But when the doctors examined him prior to operating, the condition was completely healed. Although the doctors attempted to find a medical reason for the disappearance of the condition, they were unable to do so. They actually declared, "This is a miracle!"

Real miracles can be tested and confirmed.

Counterfeit Anointing

The Bible warns believers not to counterfeit the anointing of the Holy Spirit. We are not to imitate the anointing, nor are we to try to replicate miracles or the supernatural, or use it for our own purposes.

God commanded that any person who duplicated the formula of anointing oil—to be used solely in the Tabernacle—faced judgment:

> "It shall not be poured on anyone's body, nor shall you make any like it in the same proportions; it is holy, and it shall be holy to you. Whoever shall mix any like it or whoever puts any of it on a layman shall be cut off from his people."
>
> Exodus 30:32–33

The Israelites were not allowed even to imitate the smell of the anointing oil.

The supernatural power of God is authentic, and there should be no imitation of the miraculous.

The Old Testament tells the tragic story of two sons of Aaron, the high priest:

> Now Nadab and Abihu, the sons of Aaron, took their respective firepans, and after putting fire in them, placed incense on it and offered strange fire before the Lord, which He had not commanded them. And fire came out from the presence of the Lord and consumed them, and they died before the Lord.
>
> Leviticus 10:1–2

J. Lee Grady, in his "Fire in My Bones" column for *Charisma*, comments on this serious passage:

> No one fully understands what Nadab and Abihu did to prompt God to strike them dead in the sanctuary of Israel. The Bible says they loaded their firepans with incense, ignited the substance and "offered strange fire before the Lord." . . . As a result of their careless and irreverent behavior, fire came from God's presence and consumed them.
>
> Zap. In an instant they were ashes.
>
> When Moses had to explain to Aaron what happened to the two men, he said: "It is what the Lord spoke, saying, 'By those who come

near to Me I will be treated as holy, and before all the people I will be honored'" (v. 3). Although we don't know the details of what Nadab and his brother did with the holy incense, we know they were careless and irreverent about the things of God.[3]

Many false prophets and teachers start out as genuine men and women of God. They have hearts turned toward the Lord. Somewhere along the way, however, they fail to guard their hearts. They are careless and irreverent. A mixture—"unauthorized fire"—comes in. It may start with a "simple" exaggeration of their stories. The stories are so sensational that large crowds come to hear them and see similar supernatural occurrences.

I read a story about a woman in the 1970s who testified that both her breasts had been removed in a double mastectomy. The crowds were mesmerized as she described the cancer spreading to her brain and to almost every organ in her body. The woman continued that both breasts had been restored one night while she was sleeping. Her powerful story detailed the complete healing of her body. Not only were her breasts restored, but there were no scars left from her mastectomy!

The problem with this story was that the woman never had cancer.

You might think that when her story was revealed to be false, believers would have been eager to find out the truth. But leaders and laypersons alike were accused of a lack of faith when they did not believe her story. They were also accused of being on a witch hunt.[4]

How sad that thousands of believers had been deceived by this woman because the fraudulent story was never tested and examined!

Judge Only the Fruit

It is not possible, as we said at the beginning of this chapter, to judge the motives of a person's heart. A person can also have a heart for the Lord and still be deceived—ignorant of the biblical principles for the operation of the supernatural. When we are judging the supernatural, then, we are to evaluate the outward fruit and not the motives of the heart so that we are not deceived. Jesus said,

> "Beware of the false prophets, who come to you in sheep's clothing, but inwardly are ravenous wolves. You will know them by their fruits. Grapes are not gathered from thorn bushes nor figs from thistles, are they? So every good tree bears good fruit, but the bad tree bears bad fruit."
>
> Matthew 7:15–17

Not only are we not to judge a person's heart, but we are not to judge personality or style. We are to judge only the fruit being produced.

Believers also need to test what is being preached. Does it line up with Scripture, or is it some "private revelation" not found in the Bible? Does the teaching produce bad fruit such as rebellion to authority or pride? Does it draw people away from the local church? Or, on the other hand, does it produce the fruit of God's Spirit?

> The fruit of the Spirit is love, joy, peace, patience, kindness, goodness, faithfulness, gentleness, self-control; against such things there is no law.
>
> Galatians 5:22–23

Even though the enemy is able to counterfeit the voice of God and His leading, we have a promise from the Lord: "My sheep hear My voice, and I know them, and they follow Me" (John 10:27).

Since I grew up in a church that told me God does not speak today, I often say, "I'm not sure when God lost His voice!" His Word promises that we are able to hear Him speak and that we can know His voice. As we fellowship with Him through the power of His Holy Spirit, we are able to recognize His voice.

Before Dale and I were married, we were living about 1,500 miles apart. When he called on the phone, I was able to recognize his voice from his first few words, before he could tell me who was calling. We had spent time together. We had shared our thoughts and dreams for the future. We knew each other's hearts. If a person had told me something about Dale that did not line up with his character, I could easily reject the message. Why? Because I knew him!

We are able to do the same thing with the Lord. Spending time with Him, knowing Him through the Scriptures and by the empowering of His Spirit helps us judge whether a supernatural miracle or message is from God or evil spirits.

In the following chapter we will look at various ways to guard against deception.

Prayer

Heavenly Father, thank You for helping me to judge righteously. Forgive me for those times I have ignored Your promptings, in order to avoid judging. I now accept my responsibility to be a spiritual person and to judge all things. Create within me a deep desire to walk in Your presence so that I will be alert to deceptive spirits. With Your help I will guard my heart from any mixture or exaggeration so I can have a clean heart before You. Thank You, Lord, for Your Holy Spirit, who will lead me into all truth. In Jesus' name I pray, Amen.

For Further Reflection

1. Why is the teaching that Christians are not to judge a dangerous doctrine?
2. What are some of the ways a believer can judge the supernatural?
3. What are the three parts of man's being, and what role does each play in judging the supernatural?
4. What part of a human being rightly judges the supernatural?
5. Describe a time when you sensed inside that something was wrong. What happened?

6

Guarding against Deception

Katie had been a friend of mine. We had ministered together for several years. She had one of the most powerful prophetic gifts I have ever witnessed. She had a good education, and she and her husband, a successful businessman, had three beautiful children and a lovely home. They seemed like the ideal American family. She was even reaching the country club set with the Gospel. Life seemed good!

After a few years, however, something changed. Katie began receiving frequent "visitations" from Jesus. Katie's prophetic words now carried a judgmental edge. And she was isolating herself from other believers. No longer could she fellowship with the Body of Christ, she said, since she and Jesus needed time alone. She said He would visit her in the middle of the night and, standing at the foot of her bed, would wash her feet. She could not attend church in her town since no church was "spiritual" enough.

Another minister friend and I felt we needed to reach out and encourage her to come out of isolation so she could fellowship with other believers. As we visited with her at her home one evening, we expressed our concern and love for her.

Katie stared at both of us and exclaimed, "How dare you question that I can hear the Lord?"

My minister friend and I were shocked and saddened by this response.

From that point on, Katie refused to answer our phone calls or letters. We continued to hear strange reports from those who had followed her ministry for years. Everyone seemed concerned. She was waking her children in the middle of the night and taking them around the city to pray with an attitude of aggressive spiritual warfare. She continued to release prophetic words in a harsh tone and with strong words of judgment against the Body of Christ. The path of deception was taking Katie further and further from the truth.

It was not long until Katie's husband divorced her. She lost custody of her beautiful children and even her grip on sanity.

Years later Katie's sister attended one of my meetings. She gave me a sad report about Katie going into the apartment parking lot where she was living. After beating all the cars with a baseball bat, she called the police and ended up temporarily in jail.

How tragic! What a loss to her family! What a loss to the Body of Christ! How could something like this happen? How could a person with such a powerful anointing on her life sink to such a tragic place? And are there ways for believers to guard themselves against the deceptive tactics of the enemy?

Thankfully, the answer is yes.

Be a Berean Believer

One of the ways the enemy gains a foothold into the lives of believers is through their desire to draw closer to God. The enemy is able to come in cunning ways to give supernatural experiences and speak godly sounding words in order to trap these believers into believing they actually *are* getting nearer to God.

Katie thought she was having supernatural experiences with Jesus. She heard words telling her she was more spiritual than other Christians, that no church in town could understand the spiritual things she knew. Katie continued to pull away from people and spend time alone so she could draw even closer to God. The enemy had seen her God-ward desires and used them for her ruin.

Being a good Christian is no guarantee of freedom from deception. Guarding against deception, then, should be a high priority in the life of a believer. Becoming a Berean believer, as we saw in the introduction, is one of the first ways to help protect us from the tactics of the enemy.

> These were more noble-minded than those in Thessalonica, for they received the word with great eagerness, examining the Scriptures daily to see whether these things were so.
>
> Acts 17:11

The Bereans tested what they heard. They checked out teaching against the Scriptures to see if the teaching was in agreement with the Word of God.

I have indicated that, although I was in church all my life, I did not read my Bible. I heard sermons but did not do my own Bible study. One of the first things that came to me when I was filled with the Holy Spirit was an immediate hunger for the Bible.

Some time later I was asked to lead an organization that was influencing many spiritually. I accepted, but wanted to make sure I would be leading under the direction of the Holy Spirit. One day I was praying for direction and wisdom. I asked the Lord what I needed to do to lead this organization in the way He wanted. Then I sensed the Lord speaking in my spirit. He said I was to "study to show myself approved to God." I knew this was from Scripture but had no idea where to find it. Finally I looked up the passage in a reference book: "Study to shew thyself approved unto God, a workman that needeth not to be ashamed, rightly dividing the word of truth" (2 Timothy 2:15, KJV).

This Scripture became a guiding principle for my life. At the time it made no sense to me, as I did not realize what studying the Bible had to do with leading an organization. Today I understand why the Lord spoke that to me. He was preparing me for more than an organization; He was preparing me for my future. If I was to guard against deception, I would need to check out modern-day phenomena and teaching with the Bible.

Discern the Truth

Discernment is another way for believers to guard themselves against the deceptive tactics of the enemy.

I had been taught in church that Satan was reserved for unbelievers after death. He could not affect Christians while they were alive. Then a missionary serving in a foreign country spoke at our church about the activity of demons in countries outside the United States. He recounted stories of people who were demonized and about occult activity in the country where he had been ministering. At the end of his message he made a statement not surprising for that context. "We do not have demonic activity like this in the United States," he said. "People are not demonized because we are too cultured for this to happen."

My church endorsed his message. Our belief was that American culture is exempt from demonic activity.

But that missionary was deceived! One of the first things I learned once I started reading the Bible was the reality of demons. I also learned that I could no longer listen to any teacher and merely accept the teaching as true. I had to look to God's Word to find truth. Jesus, for example, said, "Heal the sick, raise the dead, cleanse the lepers, cast out demons" (Matthew 10:8). So the Bible changed my mind about demons!

When the high priest in the Old Testament wanted to discern the truth or will of God, he used two objects. These objects were kept in the breastplate of his priestly attire. No command came from God to make the objects. Scholars do not even know what the specific objects were. The high priest was simply told to put them in the breastplate, the square of patterned brocade that covered his heart. These objects were called the Urim and the Thummim.

The *lots* or *stones* of the breastplate pouch may have been cast like sacred dice, somehow revealing by their fall the divine will or judgment of God. The practice of casting lots is found in the stories of Samuel's public choosing of Saul as king (see 1 Samuel 10:19–22) and Saul's discovery of Jonathan as the one who had violated his command (see 1 Samuel 14:36–42). The custom of casting lots in order to decide matters was common among the Hebrews and other people of antiquity. Casting lots was taken, no doubt, from the tradition of standing before the Urim and Thummim to determine the mind of the Lord in important matters.[1]

Some translators give the meanings of those Hebrew words as *lights* and *perfections*. My own understanding is that those objects represent God's Spirit and God's Word. The Holy Spirit brings light and the Word of God shows us His perfect ways. Both are invaluable tools to help us hear from the Lord and to guard against deception.

As believers, you and I are priests unto the Lord. Although we do not wear the Old Testament robes of the priesthood, we are clothed with the righteousness of Jesus Christ and the power of the Holy Spirit. Just as Old Testament saints inquired about the will of God through the Urim and Thummim, we have access to the will of God through His Spirit and His Word. How thankful I am to live in a time when we can have the Word and the Spirit dwelling continually in our hearts to help us discern the difference between truth and error!

Keep the Ministry Pure

Believers should be aware that the flesh, our carnal nature, can imitate the working of the Holy Spirit. Instances of this happening are found throughout the Bible.

Earlier we looked at the tragic corruption of the first two sons of the first high priest, Aaron, who "offered strange fire before the LORD, which He had not commanded them" (Leviticus 10:1). We must never blend the fire of the Spirit with falsehood or our own agenda.

Years ago I was ministering at a conference for leaders. The Spirit of the Lord revealed to me that a mixture was taking place at some of the meetings in the churches in that city.

I spoke out the revelation to the congregation that evening. I told them I sensed that ministers were coming into churches in that city and taking money from church members in exchange for a prophetic word. "Thus saith the Lord" would be spoken along with "prophetic words" the Lord had *not* spoken. This manipulative practice had been going on in the city for some time.

Just the previous week, a skillful leader had told the congregation that if they wanted a *great* word from the Lord, it would cost them a thousand dollars. People lined up excitedly for the thousand-dollar "prophecies." Next was the line for *good* prophecies. These people were required to give one hundred dollars each. The remainder of the people were lined up against a wall and asked a pointed question: "Where is your faith?" One widow had just received her inheritance from her recently deceased husband. She gave $25,000 in an offering for the speaker.

Some local leaders and believers were simply chalking this up to personality or style. But I admonished them to call this practice by its proper name, false prophecy, as a way to rectify these ungodly activities. If the leaders would speak the truth, call the ministry false and repent, then the Lord would open the door for genuine prophetic ministry in that city.

After I delivered this strong message, I wondered what the reaction would be. Then I saw the hostess for the conference, at which a minister friend and I were speaking, get up from her seat in the back of the room and walk toward me. She was crying and admitted that what I had spoken was true. After her confession, she asked a pastor to stand and repent on behalf of the pastors in that city who had allowed this bogus prophetic ministry to take place in their churches. Afterward my minister friend and I prayed and prophesied over every person in the meeting. The ministry over about four hundred individuals went nonstop until three in the morning.

Not one penny changed hands. We were breaking the power of the prophetic curse holding back a move of the true prophetic voice of God for that city. Believers started to realize they did not need to give money in order to receive a word from God. The gifts of God are freely given. "Freely you received, freely give" (Matthew 10:8). No manipulation or control! Once repentance took place, a true anointing from God was released to break the power of the unholy mixture of flesh with the Holy Spirit.

We Cannot Earn God's Favor

Although we are surprised at the idea of buying prophetic words, payment for spiritual advancement is not new. The selling of indulgences—in a sense, buying time off from purgatory—was a catalyst for the Protestant Reformation almost five hundred years ago. Their sale was subsequently outlawed by the Roman Catholic Church. But in 2000 Pope John Paul II authorized indulgences—to be earned, not bought—as part of the celebration of the third millennium. His successor, Pope Benedict XVI, has made indulgences available even more frequently as part of church anniversary celebrations. From a recent *New York Times* news article:

> According to church teaching, even after sinners are absolved in the confessional and say their Our Fathers or Hail Marys as penance, they still face punishment after death, in Purgatory, before they can enter heaven. In exchange for certain prayers, devotions or pilgrimages in special years, a Catholic can receive an indulgence, which reduces or erases that punishment instantly, with no formal ceremony or sacrament.

91

There are partial indulgences, which reduce purgatorial time by a certain number of days or years, and plenary indulgences, which eliminate all of it, until another sin is committed. You can get one for yourself, or for someone who is dead. You cannot buy one—the church outlawed the sale of indulgences in 1567—but charitable contributions, combined with other acts, can help you earn one. There is a limit of one plenary indulgence per sinner per day.[2]

Contrast this approach to salvation with Ephesians 2:8–9: "By grace you have been saved through faith; and that not of yourselves, it is the gift of God; not as a result of works, so that no one may boast."

We Must Guard against Manipulation

Deceitful practices such as what had been happening in those churches are sometimes referred to as *charismatic witchcraft*. Witchcraft is any effort to employ ungodly means to dominate, control or manipulate others. Witchcraft can infiltrate the Church and be used against unsuspecting Christians. Listen to the warning of the apostle Peter:

> Many will follow their destructive ways, because of whom the way of truth will be blasphemed. By covetousness they will exploit you with deceptive words; for a long time their judgment has not been idle, and their destruction does not slumber.
>
> 2 Peter 2:2–3, NKJV

Rick Renner writes about this Scripture and spiritual manipulation:

> The word *covetousness* is from the Greek word *pleonexia* (pleo-nex-ia), and is used throughout the New Testament to denote an *insatiable greed* or a *strong desire for more, more, more and more. . . .*
>
> It is also interesting that when Peter wrote about *covetousness* in this verse, he wrote in the locative tense. This tells us that false prophets and false teachers function *totally* from a greedy vantage

point. In fact, they are *locked in a sphere of greed* and do everything they do with one thing in mind: *how will this profit me?*

By looking at the word *pleonexia*, we discover what it is that these false revelators are primarily after. The word *pleonexia* (*covetousness*) is primarily used in Greek literature to denote an *insatiable desire* for 1) *more money*, 2) *more power*, or 3) *more influence.*[3]

Our spirits must be alive and fully sensitive to the Holy Spirit in order to guard against such manipulation.

Guard Your Heart

Not only do we need to maintain the purity of the ministry, but remember that we cannot trust our own hearts. Anyone who denies that he or she is capable of being deceived is deceived already. Our hearts are incapable of distinguishing truth from error. "He who trusts in his own heart is a fool" (Proverbs 28:26).

Recall, too, the warning of the prophet Jeremiah that the heart cannot be trusted: "The heart is more deceitful than all else and is desperately sick; who can understand it?" (Jeremiah 17:9).

But keeping our hearts clean from bitterness, unforgiveness, pride and other sins helps guard against deception.

Live a Righteous Life

Our hearts and lives need to be separated unto God. I am not talking about religious elitism, but about not compromising with the world. We live in the world but must not allow the corruption of the world to be part of us. The Spirit of God and the trappings of the world are in opposition to each other:

> Now we have received, not the spirit of the world, but the Spirit who is from God, so that we may know the things freely given to us by God.
>
> 1 Corinthians 2:12

The early Church was aware of those who believed they could live their lives separate from God's principles found in Scripture. Those erring believers thought that salvation was for the soul only. Gnostics and others taught a heresy called *antinomianism*, which means "opposed to law." Those who endorsed this doctrine denied that the principles found in God's Word should directly control the believer's life. In fact, they said that a person could behave in an unrestrained way and it did not matter. *Spiritual antinomianism*, the total opposite of legalism, concluded that a person did not need to be taught by God's Word on how to live but could rely on inner promptings.

Antinomianism also taught that God does not see sin in a believer's life. Since that person is in Christ, his or her behavior makes no difference to the Lord. This belief is correct in saying that man is saved by faith alone. The error, however, is the statement that man is free from the law and is no longer bound to obey the principles of God's Word.

I read somewhere that law without love is Pharisaism; love without law is antinomianism. Too often we find Christians living the same way as unbelievers. Since man is no longer accountable for living a life directed by the Scriptures, the influence of Christians in society has diminished.[4]

Some believers even today say that since we are living in a period of grace and not law, keeping the commandments as presented by religious authorities, therefore, is not required. The only law believers are required to keep, they believe, is the law of love. "Do we then nullify the Law through faith? May it never be! On the contrary, we establish the Law" (Romans 3:31).

Jewish converts thought they had to keep the Law, but the apostle Paul explained to them that the Law had "died" and that they were free from it. The purpose of the Law is not to motivate or change us, he said, but rather to reveal sin and our need for Christ. We are to serve God from a motivation of love and not law.

Paul went on to argue that it is vain to look for justification by the works of the law. It is only by faith, he said, that a man is justified apart from "good works." Justification can be obtained without the keeping of Moses' Law, and this is called the righteousness of God, which we don't earn but which He confers on us. The principle of faith makes it impossible for us to boast in our own ability to save ourselves through good works. Although believers are justified by faith, we are not left lawless. Faith is a different, higher law. Jesus, through His life and death, completely obeyed the demands of the Law.

The doctrine of justification by faith is not against the law, then, because it establishes the law. Christ's righteousness is given to believers by faith alone. His righteousness causes a new heart to be formed within us. And the creation of a new heart—thank God!—produces changes in conduct and temper.

Have a Mentor

Keeping our hearts clean and living a life of righteousness are musts, but having a good mentor will also help us guard against the deception of the enemy.

The business world uses the word *coach* for a similar function. Ted Engstrom in his book *The Fine Art of Mentoring* points out that the word *mentor* actually comes from Greek mythology. In Homer's *Odyssey*, Ulysses asks a wise man named Mentor to care for his son while Ulysses is fighting in the Trojan War. Apparently Mentor, a trusted counselor, is successful in his responsibilities. The son he cares for grows up to be a fine young man and even helps his father recover his kingdom.[5]

Having the right mentor is vital for your life. Allow the Lord to lead you to the one who is right for you. Often you will sense an attraction to that person. Not only should you be drawn to the mentor, but the mentor must also be drawn to you.

My friend apostle John Kelly often says, "Don't ever let anyone cover you who does not love you." I agree! You do not need to align with someone who is on a power trip and feeding his or her own ego. Look for a person who wants you to succeed.

In an earlier book I wrote:

> One of the ways to be sure that you and your potential mentor are heading in the same direction is by asking yourself if you view this person as a worthy and reputable role model. In other words, you should be able to look at your potential mentor and see something that you would want in your own life, a *deposit* of God that you are willing to exert whatever effort is necessary to obtain for yourself. A good mentor will be more than willing to walk with you until that deposit of God is released within you.[6]

The Hebrew priests in the Old Testament were chosen, in part, to teach God's people how to know the difference between right and wrong: "They shall teach My people the difference between the holy and the profane, and cause them to discern between the unclean and the clean" (Ezekiel 44:23).

The Church needs mature and gifted leaders to train and equip believers to operate in the ability to separate the clean from the unclean, the holy from the profane. But because many believers today have not been properly taught—perhaps they are uneducated in the Word of God or they have not been trained in the workings of the Holy Spirit—they call the works of God *evil* and the works of the enemy *good*. We desperately need leaders who will train us for the decisions we must make each day.

Now let's take a look at the dangers we Christians face as the result of a malady that may surprise you.

Prayer

Thank You, Lord, for Your Word and Your Holy Spirit to help me discern the difference between the workings of Your Spirit, man's flesh and demonic spirits. Help me guard against mixing the working of Your Spirit with my own flesh. I want to walk in the pure anointing of Your Holy Spirit. Please cleanse my heart of any unforgiveness, pride, bitterness or any other sin. I reject all charismatic witchcraft that would try to manipulate me, and I will not try to manipulate others. With Your help, I fully embrace Your gift of righteousness. Thank You for giving me a new heart and the grace to live a life that is pleasing to You. In Jesus' name, Amen.

For Further Reflection

1. Give your own definition of being a "Berean believer."
2. Why is it important?
3. Why is it important to understand the activity of demons on the earth?
4. What is the present-day meaning of *Urim* and *Thummim*?
5. What are the three things false prophets and false teachers want?

7

Dangers of Passivity
and Spiritual Boredom

Donald had been fasting for more than forty days with no food and no water. He had become so weak that he was having trouble walking to the bathroom.

Dale and I were Donald's pastors at that time. Several members of our church had expressed concern that Donald would die if he did not stop fasting.

I had not slept for several nights as I prayed for him. I interceded for his health and asked the Lord for wisdom in dealing with the situation. Then Dale and I decided to visit Donald at his home.

After his wife invited us in, we found him lying on a pad on the floor. His color was gray, his eyes were dull, and he was having difficulty sitting up or even talking. We expressed our concern and told him that, as his pastors, we felt it was time for him to end his fast.

Donald replied that he had not heard from God to end his fast and that he would not do so unless he did. The Lord had told him, he said, to do a total fast. He said God had told him when he was to begin the fast and that He would tell him when to end it. But Donald could not tell us why he was fasting. He was doing it in obedience to the word he had heard, and he said he felt responsible to the Lord to be obedient.

After trying to reason with Donald, Dale and I gave him a choice: Either end the fast, or we as the church leaders would let the congregation know we were no longer responsible for him. But after much talking and trying to reason, I sensed that Donald needed a firmer word to help him face reality.

"If this is not God's time for you to end the fast," I said, "I will be responsible to God for your decision. As your pastor, I will take responsibility for urging you to do this."

Suddenly Donald seemed open to what I was saying. He consulted with his wife. She urged him to listen to us and do what we were asking.

Finally Donald agreed to our counsel. We asked his wife to bring him a glass of juice and have him drink a few sips while we were there. He agreed. And by the time we left, he was on the path to recovery.

Donald had become deceived by allowing his mind to become passive. He failed to reason with the voice he had heard. He could identify no purpose in his fast. He was merely listening to and obeying a voice that had pressured him to obey without seeing any good fruit from the action.

Variations of Passivity

Donald's may be an extreme example, but as we have seen, all believers are susceptible to deception.

Surrendering Your Will

When believers surrender their wills to God, they will be deceived if they make the mistake of becoming robots. God does not over-power or take away a person's will. The enemy, on the other hand, loves to capture the person's will and use it for his own evil purposes. Usually the enemy gives him or her a wrong interpretation of Scrip-ture. This causes the person to think he is obeying God's Word when he is actually obeying the leading of evil spirits.

One of the Scriptures the enemy uses against Christians is Phi-lippians 2:13: "It is God who is at work in you, both to will and to work for His good pleasure." God desires for humans to exercise their wills. (We talked in chapter 5 about the *soul* being made up of the mind, will and emotions.) "I urge you, brethren," wrote Paul, "by the mercies of God, to present your bodies" (Romans 12:1). That happens by an exercise of the will.

When Jesus saves a person, the power of God is at work to help him or her make right choices. But the enemy tries to get that person to forgo choosing and, under the guise of submitting his or her will to God's will, to become passive.

Having a Meek Spirit

The enemy knows Scripture and how to twist its meaning to get a person off track. He will use a Scripture like the following to convince a believer to become passive in his will:

> Let [your adornment] be the hidden person of the heart, with the imperishable quality of a gentle and quiet spirit, which is precious in the sight of God.
>
> 1 Peter 3:4

The enemy equates a meek and quiet spirit (when the person believes he has surrendered his will to God) to passivity. But when we read this verse in context with the next few verses, we see that a "quiet spirit" coexists with the active exercise of the will. "Do what is right without being frightened by any fear," continues Peter (verse 6). The deceived believer, however, fails to choose what is right or determine an action or act from his or her will.

Such passivity, surprising as this is, is actually similar to some of the ideas found in Hindu spirituality. Hinduism's belief in reincarnation is connected with the inevitability of one's fate. What will happen is determined by *karma*—the effects of a person's actions that determine his destiny in his next incarnation—resulting in either acceptance and detachment or futility and hopelessness. Either reaction can result in passivity.

And the "four main pathways" to spirituality in Hinduism stand in stark contrast to the teaching of Jesus, who stated, "I am the way, and the truth, and the life; no one comes to the Father but through Me" (John 14:6). There is only one pathway, and we must lay hold of it.

Identifying with Jesus' Suffering

Another aspect of passivity sometimes occurs in the area of identifying with the sufferings of Jesus. I have heard many devout Christians say that the physical illness in their bodies is for the purpose of identifying with the sufferings of the Lord. Some even embrace cancer or another devastating illness as a means of suffering with Him. Or they believe they are suffering for other people—perhaps for their healing or salvation—or vicariously for the Body of Christ. Some Christians actually see themselves as martyrs and go through extreme anguish in their spirits or pain in their bodies.

These deceived believers do not understand that they are actually victims of deceiving spirits. There is no positive outcome as a result of the suffering caused by these demonic spirits. The person does not grow spiritually, experience victory or produce good spiritual fruit.

We suffer with Jesus only when we are rejected for the sake of the Gospel or when we are persecuted for bearing His name.

On the cross Jesus Christ "was pierced through for our transgressions, He was crushed for our iniquities; the chastening for our well-being fell upon Him, and by His scourging we are healed" (Isaiah 53:5). At the end He said, "It is finished!" (John 19:30). You and I are not worthy to suffer and make atonement for sin, nor do we need to. Jesus has done it once for all.

We will see a few more examples of this deception in the next chapter.

Becoming Tricked

Believers in a passive state can become what the Bible calls *bewitched*. "You foolish Galatians, who has bewitched you . . . ?" (Galatians 3:1). I appreciate what Rick Renner writes about the Galatian church being infiltrated by deception:

> Notice, first of all, that Paul calls them "O foolish Galatians." The word "foolish" is the Greek word *anoetos* (a-no-e-tos) and it describes "a person who acts without thinking, reasoning" or "using his or her mind." . . .
>
> Paul's strong language tells us that this church had come under some type of demonic spell and the church, as a whole, had entered into the world of foolishness.[1]

False teachers will try to convince believers they are not to reason with their minds but to accept what they are hearing and seeing without question.

What is the alternative to these variations of passivity?

A Renewed Mind

Believers need sharp, active minds in their service to the Lord, minds that are able to reason and make decisions:

I urge you, brethren, by the mercies of God, to present your bodies a living and holy sacrifice, acceptable to God, which is your spiritual service of worship. And do not be conformed to this world, but be transformed by the renewing of your mind, so that you may prove what the will of God is, that which is good and acceptable and perfect.

Romans 12:1–2

The enemy nurtures passivity in order to elicit a compulsory action from the believer. This passive mind causes the person to be guided by what he or she believes is a higher law. This leading—outside the realm of reason—tells the person what to do and what not to do.

I remember a woman years ago talking about picking up her child from school. She said she was waiting to hear whether she was supposed to pick him up. I told her quickly that I had the answer for her: "Go pick up your child from school!" Wisdom in this situation was not rocket science.

Believers who wait for a "word" for every action fall prey to deceiving spirits. God does not remove our brains when we become Christians. He causes us, rather, to be mentally even sharper because of the empowering of the Holy Spirit. The man on the extended fast whom I described at the beginning of this chapter was being guided by this so-called higher law. For a while he refused to listen to reason from others—although thankfully, he did so at last. His mind was closed to reasoning; he was waiting for a word to receive direction.

Some believers think they have heard the Lord tell them the time when Jesus is coming back. These people become passive and either quit their jobs or refuse to plan for the future.

A man I knew years ago fell into this kind of deception. He had a profitable business selling audio equipment and supplies to churches and ministries. They were able to get what they needed to record church services, conferences and a variety of other activities, at a reasonable cost and in a timely manner. The business was prospering.

But after a few years, the business owner received what he thought was a revelation from the Lord. He heard when Jesus was coming back and that he needed to shut down his business. As a result, the Body of Christ was no longer able to use his services and the man himself pitched into financial difficulty.

Since those days, technology has reached new levels. Today that man would be using and marketing CDs, DVDs, PowerPoint presentations and many other tools that were not available when he quit his business. Today Jesus still has not returned. The man missed the best for his business because of deception.

Books have been published over the years with the revelation of the date of Jesus' return. "But of that day and hour no one knows," said Jesus, "not even the angels of heaven, nor the Son, but the Father alone" (Matthew 24:36). Again, this is not rocket science!

I love what my friend apostle Jim Hodges says about the Second Coming of Jesus. He says he knows exactly when Jesus is coming: "He is coming at the appointed time. Not only that, but Jesus is coming at the end!" May we all accept that revelation and not fall into the deception of thinking it is possible for a few special people to know when Jesus is coming.

Our minds must be renewed and kept active, and with the help of the Holy Spirit we can choose the will of God in every situation.

God created His people as supernatural beings. Since we were created by a supernatural God, we have a desire for the supernatural. What a sad state the Church is in when we are so spiritually hungry for a move of God that we are willing to abandon our minds, reason, wills and even Scripture in order that we may experience spiritual power.

Spiritual Power

As believers function in the supernatural power of God, boredom and passivity are no longer issues. The supernatural should be a normal experience for all believers, who need to be equipped so they are no longer gullible to believe every supernatural experience or teaching they encounter.

Spiritual Gifts

Believers must be taught and activated in the gifts of the Holy Spirit. Paul admonished Christians not to be ignorant of spiritual gifts and their operation: "Concerning spiritual gifts, brethren, I do not want you to be unaware" (1 Corinthians 12:1).

I have recounted that, although I grew up as a faithful member of my church, I was ignorant of the Holy Spirit and His gifts. During church services we often sang the first, second and fourth verses of the hymns from the hymnal. I think the reason we skipped the third verse was because it was usually about the Holy Spirit! Since we knew little about the Spirit, we were not going to sing about Him. We sang what we knew, listened to a sermon and went home.

In all those years I was unaware that the Holy Spirit was given to believers so that we could do the work of the ministry. When I received the empowering of the Spirit as an adult, my entire life changed. My hunger for the Word of God (as I have said) caused me to devour the Bible and spend hours each day in prayer. While reading the Bible, I discovered that the Lord wants every believer to operate in the supernatural:

> "These signs will accompany those who have believed: in My name they will cast out demons, they will speak with new tongues; they will pick up serpents, and if they drink any deadly poison, it will not hurt them; they will lay hands on the sick, and they will recover."
>
> Mark 16:17–18

Although I was unaware of what God was doing in the earth, God had been restoring the power of the Holy Spirit to His Church for many years.

A significant outpouring of the Spirit, as you probably know, happened at the beginning of the twentieth century. Pentecostal fire started with a handful of students during a prayer meeting at a Bible school in Topeka, Kansas, in 1901 and swept to Azusa Street in Los Angeles in 1906 and, from there, around the world. Thousands of Pentecostal denominations were birthed during the twentieth century until they have become the largest family of Protestants in the world.[2]

This movement was born in what I call a *power rain*, when fearful and awesome manifestations and demonstrations of the Holy Spirit occur.

Power Rains

Power rains—the outpouring of supernatural manifestations of the Holy Spirit—scare people, and many are unwilling or uninterested to receive such mighty power. Not everyone embraces a fresh move of the Holy Spirit.

During the first half of the twentieth century, Pentecostals were considered a very small minority in the Church. They were misunderstood and had little impact on society. As a result, some groups and denominations moved away from their Pentecostal roots and accepted a more moderate move of the Spirit. This more moderate move, starting about 1960, became known as the charismatic movement, and it came to prominence during the Jesus movement explosion in the 1970s. Charismatics currently make up approximately 25 percent of all Christendom and are the second-largest branch of Christianity after the Roman Catholic Church.

In recent decades God has been once again pouring out the Holy Spirit and empowering believers with supernatural gifts. When the Spirit manifests His presence, saints do not suffer from spiritual boredom! Religion is boring, but Jesus and His power are never dull. There may be difficult days, but boredom while walking in the power of the Holy Spirit is never a problem.

Ascension Gift Ministries

Not only has the Lord been restoring His power to believers, but He is restoring fivefold ministry to the Church:

> He gave some as apostles, and some as prophets, and some as evangelists, and some as pastors and teachers, for the equipping of the saints for the work of service, to the building up of the body of Christ.
>
> Ephesians 4:11–12

The fivefold ministries of apostles, prophets, evangelists, pastors and teachers are sometimes referred to as *ascension gift ministries* since they were given after Jesus ascended to the Father. These gifts that Jesus gave the Church when He ascended have been restored in order to equip every believer for the work of the ministry.

Those who minister with these gifts equip other believers by teaching, activating, mentoring and maturing them to operate in supernatural ministry. Today God is using *ordinary* people to do *extraordinary* signs, wonders and miracles. Boring? Not a chance.

Doing the Works of Jesus

For the believer to exercise spiritual gifts and walk free from deception, he or she needs to be connected with mature leaders and not live in isolation. God created His people for relationship: "The Lord God said, 'It is not good for the man to be alone; I will make him a helper suitable for him'" (Genesis 2:18). Being in relationship with mature leaders and with other believers will sharpen the exercise of spiritual gifts and enable the believer to grow up in his or her God-given purpose.

Christians were created to do good works: "We are His workmanship, created in Christ Jesus for good works, which God prepared beforehand so that we would walk in them" (Ephesians 2:10).

Every Christian is also entitled to the inheritance purchased by Jesus when He died on the cross. After His ascension, the disciples taught the Scriptures and the words of Jesus. But when the Day of Pentecost arrived, and the Holy Spirit was poured out on the believers, they acted in faith on the words they had heard and actually did "the works" and the "greater works" of Jesus that He said they would do (John 14:12).

The Word of God informs us that we should be functioning in supernatural ministry. We can use our faith to activate the gifts of the Holy Spirit and do the greater works of Jesus. This is part of our inheritance as His followers.

When we actively demonstrate the power of the Spirit, we will not be drawn quickly to what is false. Spiritual boredom will be replaced by demonstrations of God's great healing, delivering and prophetic power. Ask the Lord to help you avoid the deception of passivity and align you with the fivefold ministry gifts that will teach, train and activate you for a release of His true supernatural power.

Understanding deceptive practices that have been exhibited in the past—since supernatural power is seen throughout history—helps God's people realize that the enemy is simply using his old tricks. He does not need to come up with new strategies to deceive believers as long as the old ones are still working. We will take a look at some of these deceptive strategies in the next chapter.

Prayer

Thank You, Lord, for the power of Your Holy Spirit. I choose to walk with an active mind that has been renewed by the Word of God. Jesus, I believe that You bore all of the suffering for my well-being so that I can be free. Thank You for bearing my sicknesses and my iniquities on the cross. Only You are worthy to do that! I receive an activation of the spiritual gifts that You purchased for me. I choose to allow the Holy Spirit to use me

*in supernatural power to heal the sick and perform miracles
for Your glory. In Jesus' name, Amen.*

For Further Reflection

1. How does the enemy use a passive will to bring a person into bondage?
2. Describe what it means in the biblical sense to have a meek and quiet spirit.
3. What does it mean to identify with the sufferings of Jesus?
4. Describe how a passive mind can be guided by what the person believes to be a higher law.
5. Why do believers need to be activated in the operation of spiritual gifts?

8

Deceptive Practices throughout History

During a wonderful time worshiping the Lord in a church service in a town about four hours from Oklahoma City, I opened my eyes to see an unusual sight. Although the person parading across the front of the church was dressed in feminine attire, I realized that he was a male. *Is he a transvestite?* I wondered.

He was certainly not interested in receiving help from the ushers. He wanted only to be noticed and on full display at the front of the auditorium. When the ushers were unable to get him to listen, they walked him quietly to the back of the church so he would not disrupt the service. When he was no longer able to attract the attention of the worshipers, he finally left the building.

On my way back to the hotel after the service, the driver from the church told me that the man had told the usher that he was Jesus Christ from Oklahoma City.

That deceived man—for whom Christ died—is among millions of individuals around the world living lives of deception in many different ways. Although we hear more reports of deceived people today in our interconnected and shrinking world, deception is not new to our generation. The media merely makes us more aware of it. Deception can be traced back to the Garden of Eden, as we have seen, and has occurred throughout history.

The deceptive doctrines and manifestations we are witnessing today are the same fraudulent ideas that have been present since the beginning. They simply have different names to capture the gullible and spiritually hungry.

Trying to Match God's Power

Adam was created with an ability to operate like God with a high level of supernatural power. After the Fall—caused by deception—mankind did not lose the potential for that power; it was merely immobilized. But Satan wants to corrupt the supernatural power that has been locked up in mankind and use it for his own evil purposes.

We discussed at some length in chapter 5 that we were created for the body and soul to submit to the spirit. But since the Fall, the spirit has submitted to the dominion of the flesh. The Bible tells us, "God looked on the earth, and behold, it was corrupt; for all flesh had corrupted their way upon the earth" (Genesis 6:12). Only through the power of the Holy Spirit can mankind use his supernatural power for God's purposes.

Recall that when God was ready to pour out His anointing oil on His priests, He would not allow the oil to be prepared apart from the Tabernacle or "poured on anyone's body" (Exodus 30:32) other than Aaron, the High Priest, or his sons. The anointing oil was a "type" of the Holy Spirit, who would later be poured out "on all mankind" (Joel 2:28) to empower the human spirit to bring the flesh once again under control. The oil of the Spirit? Not to be misused!

In the Old Testament, Moses used God's power against the magicians in Egypt. Exodus 7–11 records the many demonstrations of supernatural power. At first the magicians were able to demonstrate power of equal magnitude. They reached a place, however, where their demonically originated power was not able to match the power of God:

> The magicians tried with their secret arts to bring forth gnats, but they could not; so there were gnats on man and beast. Then the magicians said to Pharaoh, "This is the finger of God."
>
> Exodus 8:18–19

People operating in the evil power of the enemy come to a place where they are unable to distinguish between good and evil. They believe all supernatural power is from God and is good, without considering the source. The magicians of Egypt needed a demonstration of a power greater than their own sorcery to cause them to see God's power!

Throughout Israel's journey through the wilderness, God demonstrated His strength. He led His people with a pillar of fire by night and a pillar of cloud by day. He provided supernatural food by means of manna for His people to eat, and water from rock or springs, miraculously provided in the desert, to quench their thirst. He even flew in quail when their appetites cried out for meat.

Later, by God's power, Daniel, the Hebrew in Babylon, was able to interpret the dream of King Nebuchadnezzar when the magicians could not (see Daniel 4). Although the king's diviners possessed supernatural power, they were unable to demonstrate the same level of power Daniel possessed.

Human beings tend to interpret the release of supernatural power as being from God when, in fact, Satan may be releasing it. Many false religions release supernatural power through their followers, just as Pharaoh and Nebuchadnezzar did.

Denying the Flesh

Babylonianism, Buddhism, Taoism, the New Age movement and many other religions or philosophies have attempted to overcome the flesh for greater expressions of supernatural power. They provide instruction to adherents to destroy the hindrances of the body. The followers of these philosophies learn to unite the spirit and the soul, or they may work at strengthening the soul through training in an attempt to overcome the body. Whatever method is used, it is always for the purpose of subduing the flesh and releasing soul power from within.[1]

Supernatural power is released for performing miracles and healing sickness and disease. In the practice of Buddhism, adherents who take monastic vows involve themselves with various kinds of abstinence and ascetic practices. Monks abstain from marriage and from meat. They follow rules of conduct, including living an austere life focused on the study of Buddhist doctrine, the practice of meditation and the development of good moral character. When monks reach a more advanced, enlightened state, they can predict the future and perform supernatural wonders by magic.

The Christian Science movement, founded in the nineteenth century by Mrs. Mary Baker Eddy, teaches that there is no such thing as sickness, pain, evil and death because matter itself is unreal. Followers are taught to exercise their minds against any sickness or pain and they will be healed. Many people opposed this teaching when it was first given. Yet when doctors examined those claiming to be cured, they could not deny the healings. Recipients had tapped into false supernatural power that produced miracles.

Some followers today die after choosing Christian Science care over medical treatment. Mary Baker Eddy herself, who believed that "awakened thought" was enough to prevent death, died in 1910 at the age of 89. Still, some continue to follow her teachings today due to the deceptive supernatural power they experience.

"Spiritual" Experiences

The New Testament Church was not exempt from false supernatural manifestations. False teachers and prophets manipulated spiritually hungry believers with wild stories about unproven trips to heaven, new ideas about angels and new doctrines not found in Scripture. Hungry individuals were persuaded to fall away from sound doctrine and engage in unwholesome obsessions with weird experiences.

The apostle Paul was aware of the inroads into the infant Church being made by these false ministers. He warned the believers in strong terms to wake up and realize the danger around them:

> See to it that no one takes you captive through philosophy and empty deception, according to the tradition of men, according to the elementary principles of the world, rather than according to Christ.
>
> Colossians 2:8

When Paul admonished believers to "see to it," he was using the Greek word *blepo*. This word means "to beware as a warning."[2] The apostle was warning the Colossians to understand the warfare they were facing since danger was imminent. The enemy was about to invade the family of God and wreak havoc with their faith, bringing some into the captivity of false prophets and teachers. Tempting believers with the same bait used in the Garden of Eden with Eve, these false ministers were offering "philosophy" that would help make recipients wise, so Paul was using his apostolic authority to set the church in order.

A little further on in Colossians, he admonished believers to be cautious about those claiming supernatural experiences:

Let no one keep defrauding you of your prize by delighting in self-abasement and the worship of the angels, taking his stand on visions he has seen, inflated without cause by his fleshly mind.

Colossians 2:18

False teachers and false prophets were trying to prove their spirituality by forcing themselves into the realm of the spirit to see visions and obtain mystical experiences. These false ministers also took pleasure in "self-abasement," a modest disguise of humility. (They had been influenced by the Gnostics.) Their appearance of humility caused sincere Christians to trust them despite their deception.

In contrast to the revelations being taught by some of those false teachers who spoke of their trips to heaven, Rick Renner describes the genuine experience:

> When Biblical characters went to heaven and recorded the events that they saw there, they did not come back talking about how their mansions were decorated. Neither can you find one scriptural account where they recorded that they had conversations with saints that had died and were waiting for them there.
>
> On the contrary, people in Scripture who were granted the privilege of seeing heaven were filled with awe and wonder "for Him that sitteth upon the throne." After seeing Jesus, high and lifted up, everything else in heaven faded in comparison to His majesty and beauty.[3]

The puffed-up individuals Paul warned against had not experienced a genuine penetration of the spirit realm at all, but simply had vivid imaginations—"inflated without cause."

Relics

The deception that infiltrated the early Church did not stop with the first century. As many believers moved further from the doctrines of the apostles, darkness entered the Church. Deception increased throughout the period of time known as the Dark Ages (the initial five hundred years following the fall of Rome in A.D. 476).

During this time, members of the clergy were supposed to be well-educated, yet many barely knew how to perform basic religious services. Although they took vows of chastity, some participated in sexual immorality. Those who held high positions enjoyed luxurious lifestyles while common people lived in poverty. Needing a way to pay for their extravagance, churchmen fabricated several corrupt ways the people could ostensibly pay for their sins. One of these was taking penitential pilgrimages to sites of relics and holy places. One such place in northern Germany owned by Frederick I, prince of Saxony, had a collection of more than seventeen thousand relics. These relics supposedly included such things as a piece of Moses' burning bush, 33 fragments of Jesus' cross and some straw from His manger. Penitent Christians could pay to see these holy objects.[4]

No records indicate that the cross of Jesus was ever preserved, even though Christians searched for its remains. During the rule of Constantine the Great, the first Christian emperor of Rome, people arose (including his own mother, who was later canonized) who believed they had found relics of the cross. Due to the sensational attention given these relics, John Calvin later commented sarcastically that if all the splinters of the cross were gathered together, they would fill a ship. He also said that three hundred people would not be able to carry the cross that one person carried to Calvary![5]

Stigmata

Although much more has been recorded about deception and supernatural phenomena during the Dark Ages, I will mention only one more example: stigmata. This phenomenon occurs when bleeding or bloody wounds appear on the bodies of individuals, especially on the hands and feet, said to represent the crucifixion wounds of Jesus Christ.

The woman minister I mentioned in chapter 3 who spread feathers on the platform also had experiences of stigmata in public meetings. The marks displayed on her body resembled the wounds on the crucified body of Christ. I believe she really thought she was experiencing the wounds of Jesus.

Instances of stigmata have been reported for more than seven hundred years. Circumstances vary from case to case, although supernatural causes have never been proven. Stigmata are primarily associated with Roman Catholicism. Many reported stigmatics are members of Catholic religious orders. The majority are female.[6] People who display stigmata usually also undergo various paranormal experiences. These can be visions, channeled messages, writings, drawings or bi-location (being in two places at the same time).[7]

Historical Notes

Prior to the thirteenth century, when the first stigmata appeared, worshipers focused on the beauty of Jesus and His ministry. After this time, they were urged to focus on the death of Jesus. Artists began to paint pictures for the first time of the crucifixion, bringing attention to Jesus' blood. Paintings depicted the suffering, pain, wounding and bleeding of the Lord. This was also the first time stigmata appeared.[8]

The first known stigmatic was St. Francis of Assisi in A.D. 1224. Witnesses who saw the marks of St. Francis after his death reported the appearance of nails with the points and the nail heads showing through the skin on both sides of the hands.

There are documented reports of between 300 and 350 other people who have experienced the same, sometimes painful condition.

Another stigmatic was Emily Bicchieri, a Dominican saint born in Italy (1238–1314). She made use of mortifications like fasting, self-scourging and wearing a hair shirt. She spent a lifetime in prayer and good works. The stigmata of the crown of thorns was impressed on her head for three days of intense suffering, during which time she claimed to be visited by several of the saints associated with the Lord's Passion. At the end of three days, the pain disappeared, but she remained devoted to the crown of thorns all her life.[9]

Padre Pio

The most famous stigmatic was Padre Pio (1887–1968). He was a man of prayer and deep devotion to Jesus. He prayed so fervently that he often went into religious trances. He was willing to suffer for the good of others. A Capuchin priest from Italy who lived a simple life, Padre Pio performed miracles and was sometimes seen in more than one place at a time.

Padre Pio, whose real name was Francesco Forgione, was made a saint in 2002. A recent survey in Italy showed that more people prayed to him than to Jesus or the virgin Mary.

Pio's first stigmata appeared only three days after he had celebrated the Feast of the Stigmata of St. Francis. In 1918 he had a vision of the wounded Christ, whose hands and feet and sides were dripping with blood. After the vision disappeared, Pio had five visible stigmata, his own hands, feet and side dripping with blood. The marks, he reported, were very painful. He experienced tremendous pain from stigmata almost daily from that time until his death fifty years later.

In 2007 a book entitled *The Other Christ, Padre Pio and Nineteenth-Century Italy*, written by historian Sergio Luzzatto, outraged many in the Catholic community. It charged that Padre Pio was a fraud. Drawing on a document found in the Vatican's archive, it revealed the testimony of a pharmacist who said that the young priest had faked his stigmata with four grams of carbolic acid that he bought in 1919. The allegations outraged Padre Pio's supporters. The Catholic Anti-Defamation League said the author was a liar and "spreading anti-Catholic libels."[10]

Therese Neumann

Therese Neumann (1898–1962) was a German Catholic mystic. One day someone told her about a young student of the priesthood who had to leave seminary due to a throat ailment. She felt such remorse that she prayed to Jesus, asking why He should alone take on all the ailments of mankind. Should she not also, in her service to Him, take on at least a small part of the agonies of others? Because Therese herself was partially paralyzed and blind, she asked that the pain of the other man be put on her.

Therese's throat began to hurt, while the young seminarian recovered. His illness had been transferred to Therese.

She continued to take on other people's sicknesses—her father's rheumatism, a woman's stomach ailment, a hospital patient's fever, a soldier's wounds, even an expectant mother's delivery pains. She took on blindness from the blind. People on crutches came to her and walked away healed. She continually asked for and received the afflictions of other people.

Therese continued this practice until one day in 1925, the day Therese of Lisieux was fully canonized as a saint in the Catholic Church, her own blindness vanished and her sight was restored. Therese Neumann said the saint had called to her and cured her.

Other healings started manifesting in Therese's body. And a remarkable phenomenon: From 1927 until her death in 1962, it was said that she ate or drank nothing except the Lord's Supper. She was on a Eucharistic fast.

In addition to these experiences of supernatural phenomena, Therese was said to have experienced stigmata in which the blood defied gravity and flowed directly upward. She also had trances during which she would repeat phrases that witnesses, including priests, recognized as ancient Aramaic, the language of Jesus.[11]

Recognize the Warfare

In contrast to the mission of Therese Neumann, Jesus is the only One worthy to carry sins and sicknesses:

> Surely our griefs He Himself bore, and our sorrows He carried; yet we ourselves esteemed Him stricken, smitten of God, and afflicted. But He was pierced through for our transgressions, He was crushed for our iniquities; the chastening for our well-being fell upon Him, and by His scourging we are healed.
>
> Isaiah 53:4–5

Since Jesus bore all our sicknesses and pains as well as our sins and iniquities—the literal Hebrew for "griefs" in verse 4 is *sicknesses*, and for "sorrows," *pains*—in His body, believers do not need anyone else to carry their afflictions for them. He has done it. It is finished.

Concerning stigmata, as I said in chapter 3, the question is not whether the sign is real but what its source is. Most stigmatics are very religious and believe they are identifying with the suffering of Jesus. My own opinion, however, is that people who believe that God produces stigmata and any pain associated with it are deceived.

The apostle Paul reminds us that we are in a war and need spiritual weapons to defeat the enemy:

> Put on the full armor of God, so that you will be able to stand firm against the schemes of the devil. For our struggle is not against flesh and blood, but against the rulers, against the powers, against the world forces of this darkness, against the spiritual forces of wickedness in the heavenly places.
>
> Ephesians 6:11–12

Not everyone has been taught about the warfare involved in deception. Many have been blinded by the enemy and ended up caught in the trap. The enemy works on the desires of innocent people in their quests for God. He disguises his evil work under the cloak of seeking to draw the person closer to God. Satan is an intelligent being and strategizes to carry out his plan of deception. In the same way that he blinded Eve in the Garden, he deceives many today by arguments and by false signs and wonders.

How sad that some Christians, so hungry for a move of God, will accept anything supernatural or bizarre as a fresh move of God! Jesus warns us about those who would arise and deceive many by their signs and wonders: "False Christs and false prophets will arise and will show great signs and wonders, so as to mislead, if possible, even the elect" (Matthew 24:24).

Once a person has been deceived and eventually learns the truth, he or she is in need of healing. Wounding from people or organizations that led the person into deception requires the healing power of the Lord. For that person once again to be able to embrace the true supernatural power of God, ministry is required to heal them and set them free. We will discuss the path of restoration in the next two chapters.

Prayer

Thank You, Lord, for providing power greater than the power of the enemy. Thank You for Your power to heal sicknesses and diseases. I reject taking into my body another person's sickness. I reject stigmata and acknowledge that You were pierced and shed Your precious blood for me. Only You are worthy to do that. Help me find my delight in You and not merely in supernatural manifestations. Empower me to follow You all the days of my life and keep my eyes focused on You. You are my reason for living! In Jesus' name I pray, Amen.

For Further Reflection

1. Describe what happened between the soul and spirit in mankind as a result of the Fall.
2. How did God use various Old Testament characters to demonstrate the supernatural power of God?
3. How do some cults and false religions cause their adherents to operate in supernatural power?
4. Why did the apostle Paul warn the Colossian church to be aware of imminent danger in the Church?
5. Describe the deception associated with stigmata.

9

Deliverance and Healing

My friend Bronwen Healy is described by many people—including me!—as a trophy of grace. Bronwen had a relatively normal childhood, a good upbringing. She went to an affluent high school and attended a fine college. Her background prepared her for a life of success. Instead she became a helpless and hopeless heroin addict and turned to prostitution to fund her addiction. Years later she found Jesus as a healing and delivering Lord.

Bronwen describes her healing experience with Jesus in her book *Trophy of Grace*:

> There was a sea of men's faces, and I was standing on the shore, and between me and them was the blood of Jesus, flowing like a waterfall. I was crying, and when I looked up, Jesus was standing high up above me. . . . With Him was an army of angels; they looked golden. He reached down and picked me up and held me

in His hands—and washed me with His precious blood. Then He wiped away my tears with the cloth of His robe. He placed me back down, and I knew that I would never be the same, I had been touched by the Holy Spirit of God.

I had received the forgiveness in my spirit that He had been so desperate to give to me: *never to be the same again!*[1]

Thousands like Bronwen have been deceived by the enemy. The enemy convinced her that his plan for her life was better than the life planned by Jesus. But the amazing grace of God stripped off the blinders so that Bronwen could see the truth.

The world today is filled with countless individuals who have been blinded by the enemy's deception. Not only are members of the Body of Christ caught in the trap of deception, but even many leaders.

> The whole head is sick and the whole heart is faint. From the sole of the foot even to the head there is nothing sound in it, only bruises, welts and raw wounds, not pressed out or bandaged, nor softened with oil.
>
> Isaiah 1:5–6

The good news is that anyone can be set free and healed by the power of the Holy Spirit.

Healing Is a Process

We are living at a time when church splits, pornography, drugs, child molestation, financial fraud and immorality are on the rise in the lives of Christians. If merely an increase in the knowledge of the Bible would cure what ails us, we would be the most wholesome generation of Christians to live on the earth! With all the teaching resources available through churches, bookstores, conferences, seminars, Bible schools and the Internet, the Word of God can be obtained as never before in history. At the same time, biblical illiteracy is on the rise!

126

An increase in the amount of traditional counseling has not solved the problem of multiplied sin either. Yet the Lord makes a way for His people to be set free and healed from the wounding caused by the deception of the enemy.

Believers often assume that when they receive Jesus as Lord of their lives, they are immediately set free from all the entanglements of the enemy. They are probably familiar with this Scripture: "If anyone is in Christ, he is a new creature; the old things passed away; behold, new things have come" (2 Corinthians 5:17).

Often we have not understood—or imparted to others—the reality that salvation is a *process*. The biblical meaning of *salvation* is "material and temporal deliverance from danger . . . ; safety; health."[2] The fullness of salvation makes provision for the person to be made whole. And eternal life is *immediate*:

> By grace you have been saved through faith; and that not of your-selves, it is the gift of God; not as a result of works, so that no one may boast.
>
> Ephesians 2:8–9

"You have been saved." It is done. Jesus' blood has washed away all your sins. His resurrection life has given you new life once you accept Him as Lord and Savior.

Yet the fullness of salvation requires a process. This process is called sanctification. Often a person still has deep wounding from the past. Usually wrong habit patterns are built into the person's life. There can also be demonic structures. These habits and structures must be broken so that the "new creature" is able to live according to the Spirit and not according to the old nature. "Walk by the Spirit," said Paul, "and you will not carry out the desire of the flesh" (Galatians 5:16). And: "Work out your salvation with fear and trembling" (Philippians 2:12).

When I accepted Jesus as Lord of my life at age twelve, I received eternal life. I have never doubted His promise of this gift. How thankful I am for this assurance! My life was controlled by various fears, however, that kept me from the fullness of life that Jesus provided in my salvation. It took many years before I received even the knowledge that my life could be different from what I had experienced. I did not understand that Jesus gave me not only eternal life, but a way for me to be set free and healed from the wounding of my past.

My spirit received eternal life in a moment, but my soul and body had to receive and walk out the promise of salvation so that my entire being could be made whole.

Healing *and* Deliverance!

We discussed in chapter 5 that mankind is made up of body, soul and spirit:

> Now may the God of peace Himself sanctify you entirely; and may your spirit and soul and body be preserved complete, without blame at the coming of our Lord Jesus Christ.
>
> 1 Thessalonians 5:23

Until we receive the healing power of the Lord in our lives, we are a product of all our yesterdays. We may respond to situations according to how we were treated, with the attitudes and opinions instilled in us as children. Adults continue to respond in childish ways until something is done to change those early patterns.

> When I was a child, I used to speak like a child, think like a child, reason like a child; when I became a man, I did away with childish things.
>
> 1 Corinthians 13:11

When a person overreacts, it shows an area that needs healing. There may be demonic influence, but it is often a manifestation of a hurt soul. Demonic deception or demonic influence in a person's life usually results in wounding that needs to be healed. All occult involvement results in a wounding of our spirits. But if deliverance is needed, that ministry must be backed up by healing, or it will not last. Healing involves not only dealing with demonic spirits but also closing the doors to the conditions that made the person vulnerable to attack in the first place.

I believe in the exorcism of demonic spirits. Several books could be written about the many people I have ministered to through the years who have been set free from the demonic. One thing I have noticed in the ministry of restoration is that there seem to be two different types of ministers—those who function in deliverance and those who function in healing.

There should be both types of ministry for the person coming out of deception. Otherwise the person is left with open wounds that caused the original wounding, and he or she can fall back into greater bruising in the future.

Arguments against Healing

In the Body of Christ we hear many arguments against healing and deliverance from past trauma. We will discuss only three of them here.

One of the arguments is that *all past sin is "under the blood"* so we do not need healing or deliverance. This understanding takes a positional view of what Jesus Christ did for us by shedding His blood at Calvary: "By one offering He has perfected for all time those who are sanctified" (Hebrews 10:14). By a person's confession of sin and receiving the forgiveness of Jesus, all his sins, and the results of those sins that might need healing or deliverance, are washed away by Jesus' blood.

The "one offering" by Jesus does indeed offer salvation to the entire world—but the entire world is not saved. A person must accept what Jesus purchased in order to receive salvation. In the same way, although healing and deliverance are available for every believer as part of salvation, not everyone has received everything Jesus purchased. We must accept and take what belongs to us. At the time of salvation, our spirits are made new. But our souls spend a lifetime getting converted!

Another argument against healing and deliverance is that *believers should not look back*. Paul did indeed recommend "forgetting what lies behind and reaching forward to what lies ahead" (Philippians 3:13). But we review what has come before, not to live in the past but to recognize sins and habit patterns that we must deal with. We discover the roots of problems so we can repent, cut those roots and be set free.

Jesus, knowing this principle, asked a question of the father whose son was mute and afflicted by seizures: "'How long has this been happening to him?' And he said, 'From childhood'" (Mark 9:21).

Jesus then rebuked the spirit and cast it out of the child. The child was made whole when the root was destroyed that had caused him and his family years of torment.

Yet another argument against healing and deliverance is that *Christians receive only blessings from God in their lives and not curses*. If a person belongs to Jesus, they say, then the devil cannot touch him or her. They believe that God's children are not vulnerable to demonic attack.

Let me be quick to say that a person who belongs to Jesus and who has the Holy Spirit living in him or her can never be possessed by a demon or by the devil! But Christians are indeed harassed by demons. Here is where the spiritual warfare of Ephesians 6 comes in. And curses exist just as surely as blessings do. Many causes of curses can be found in Scripture.

What are curses? Derek Prince defined them as words or other vehicles, including physical objects, that convey supernatural power belonging to the invisible, spiritual realm. Curses block us from receiving God's blessings in the visible realm of day-to-day events, and ultimately they shape our destiny. They may go on from generation to generation, even for thousands of years.[3] In other words, curses are the opposite of the covenantal blessings God has for His children.

Growing up in a traditional denominational church, I was given the impression that the only curses today were in the movies. Films such as *The Wizard of Oz* with the Wicked Witch of the West provided my only understanding of the reality of a curse. Years later I learned what the Bible says about curses, and the power of God to set us free from any curses that may be operating in our lives.

Paul teaches that Jesus became a curse for us: "Christ redeemed us from the curse of the Law, having become a curse for us—for it is written, 'Cursed is everyone who hangs on a tree'" (Galatians 3:13).

But we must appropriate what He did for us—in the same way we appropriate salvation—when we discover generational curses in our family line.

Is a Curse at Work?

Cults, witchcraft, Freemasonry and other deceptive systems are only counterfeits of the authentic power available to God's people. These systems and many others deceive people into believing they possess a special power within themselves and that they can arrive at some elite status above the ordinary individual.

> Let no man deceive himself. If any man among you thinks that he is wise in this age, he must become foolish, so that he may become wise. For the wisdom of this world is foolishness before God. For it is written, "He is the one who catches the wise in their craftiness."
>
> 1 Corinthians 3:18–19

The most destructive patterns in a person's life are those created by occult sins, either our own or those of past generations. But every believer can access the delivering and healing power of God. We do not need either counterfeit power or the resulting curses from it!

You can probably think of many strong believers who suffer from generational sicknesses such as diabetes, mental illness or blood pressure problems. Others have family members who suffer from adultery, poverty, drug use or divorce. Many times such roots can be traced back to former generations.

There are a number of ways to recognize if a curse is operating in your life or in your family line.

Continual frustration. One of the evidences is continual frustration. The same problems keep coming up over and over. Maybe the same problems happened in the lives of your parents or grandparents. Such patterns need to be broken.

Being accident-prone. When a young woman who attended our church years ago was involved in a car accident, I discovered that she had suffered a succession of accidents from the time she was a child—another indication that a curse may be at work. This pattern had disrupted her health, depleted her finances and caused her continual frustration.

After discussing her family history, we prayed, asking the Lord for discernment. She asked for forgiveness, not only for herself but for the sins of her parents and of former generations. We used the authority of Jesus to break the power of any and all generational curses from her life that had been activated by unconfessed sin, perhaps even by occult involvement. (The family member would not necessarily have placed a curse on upcoming generations, but opened the way through sin, at which point demonic powers would have been happy to jump in.) She broke those curses and exercised forgiveness toward any person in her family history who had opened the door in this way for a curse to operate in her life.

We sometimes call this "identificational repentance." As a family member, this young woman could choose to identify with the sin of those in her family background, confess it and put it under the blood of Jesus.

Years later she still rejoices over not having had a single accident, from the moment we prayed.

Mental or emotional breakdown. Another indication that a curse may be at work in a person's life is mental and/or emotional breakdown. Not all emotional and mental breakdowns are curses. Physical or chemical imbalance can also cause these disturbances. But when a curse is present, a pattern of emotional breakdown usually manifests itself through the generations.

Chronic sickness. A curse can also be seen through repeated or chronic sickness, especially if this is hereditary or without a clear medical diagnosis. Sometimes these conditions have medical or even psychosomatic causes. On the other hand, a curse may be in operation.

Female problems. Another indication of a curse can be repeated miscarriages or related female problems. These curses occur frequently in families that have been involved in Freemasonry. Ron G. Campbell has written an eye-opening book on the dangers of Freemasonry.

> Many have Masons in their family backgrounds and see Freemasonry as a harmless or even constructive fraternal organization. But the public is unaware of the concealed mysticism and secrecy behind closed doors of the Lodge. The secret information involves occult knowledge known as esoteric knowledge or wisdom. . . .Good men, often without realizing it, have submitted themselves to pagan gods when they have bowed their knees at the altars of Freemasonry. Some theologians say that those altars today are similar to the pagan altars of the ancient Middle East. Freemasonry is, therefore, occult in nature. . . . The roots of Freemasonry stem from a bizarre spirituality involving fertility cults and sun-god worship—forms of mythology and idolatry that have surfaced in every culture on earth and that are specifically condemned in the Bible.[4]

With the amount of Freemasonry in the United States and around the world, it is not surprising to see so many women afflicted with miscarriage and female problems. Jesus loves women! He came to set them free from all the premature death and sickness from the enemy.

Family breakdown. Many families experience an uncommon degree of breakdown and alienation. These families seem to just fall apart. Not only is there alienation and divorce but there is separation from the children. The Old Testament promises freedom from that curse:

> "Behold, I am going to send you Elijah the prophet before the coming of the great and terrible day of the LORD. He will restore the hearts of the fathers to their children and the hearts of the children to their fathers, so that I will not come and smite the land with a curse."
>
> Malachi 4:5–6

Repentance and turning to God are part of the promised restoration of family relationships. A curse destroys families, but God's love and mercy redeems and restores them!

Financial lack. Another indication of a curse is continual financial insufficiency. Even when the income should be sufficient, there is lack. The prophet Haggai spoke of a similar situation with the people of his day:

> "You have sown much, but harvest little; you eat, but there is not enough to be satisfied; you drink, but there is not enough to become drunk; you put on clothing, but no one is warm enough; and he who earns, earns wages to put into a purse with holes."
>
> Haggai 1:6

A curse was operating among God's people.

A similar situation occurred during the days of the prophet Malachi. The people were withholding their tithes and bringing defective offerings to the Lord. And the result? Because of their sin and disobedience, they had come under a curse. Their fields and vineyards were meager, since the people were essentially robbing God. Yet the Lord made a way for the curse to be broken in their lives:

> "Will a man rob God? Yet you are robbing Me! But you say, 'How have we robbed You?' In tithes and offerings. You are cursed with a curse, for

you are robbing Me, the whole nation of you! Bring the whole tithe into the storehouse, so that there may be food in My house, and test Me now in this," says the LORD of hosts, "if I will not open for you the windows of heaven and pour out for you a blessing until it overflows."

Malachi 3:8–10

Failure to tithe. Failure to give God the tithes and offerings that belong to Him brings a financial curse to the disobedient. When we give God the tithe, on the other hand, He breaks the curse, opens the windows of heaven and pours out blessing beyond measure!

Other books have been written that go into more detail and list many more causes and manifestations of curses. My purpose in this chapter is simply to make you aware that demonic deception can open a person to curses, and then to reveal the goodness of God offered through deliverance and healing.

An Honest, Humble Heart

During my first semester in nursing school, I took a valuable course entitled "How to Study." One of the key principles we were taught was this: To solve a problem, you must first realize that you *have* a problem.

To solve the problem of deception, a person must first realize that he or she is deceived. Such a realization is the first step toward deliverance and healing. Realizing that you have been caught in the trap of the enemy requires honesty and humility. It is not easy to admit that what you believed to be true is false. But a humble heart is precious in the sight of the Lord: "He leads the humble in justice, and He teaches the humble His way" (Psalm 25:9).

Related to humility is a heart full of honesty. Pride keeps a person from admitting his or her condition. To walk in freedom, a person must be a lover of truth. Jesus promised that "you will know the truth, and the truth will make you free" (John 8:32).

An honest heart hates all that stands in the way of freedom. Confessing deception, as difficult as this is, opens the door to freedom. And the Bible promises freedom to those who confess their sins: "If we confess our sins, He is faithful and righteous to forgive us our sins and to cleanse us from all unrighteousness" (1 John 1:9).[5]

Regardless of the level of deception in a person's life, God has made a way for His people to be set free. Begin by praying a prayer of release. Confess any deception that may be in your life, even if you are not sure. Then, after praying this prayer, allow the Lord to bring you into the freedom He purchased for you on Calvary. Deliverance and healing are part of your birthright as a child of God.

Prayer

Lord Jesus, I confess You as my Lord and Savior. Thank You for the freedom You purchased for me on Calvary. I commit my life to You and ask for the grace I need to walk in obedience to Your will for my life. Forgive me for my participation in sins that opened my life to deception. [Name every sin you can remember that exposed you to a curse.] Thank You for the blessings that have come to me from my ancestors. I ask that the good that came from them be filtered through the cross. I pray that the blood of Jesus flow back through my family line and wash away any ground that gives the enemy a right to my life.

The Bible says, "The Son of God appeared for this purpose, to destroy the works of the devil" (1 John 3:8). I renounce any contact with Satan, occult practices or secret societies. [Name any connections to these groups or practices.] I promise to destroy any objects associated with these groups. I command all powers of darkness to leave me and leave my family. I ask You, Father, to send angels to do battle for me.

I speak release from every generational sin or curse by

the authority I have as a child of God. Thank You, Lord, for
setting me free! In Jesus' name, Amen.

As the Lord reveals more areas of bondage, use the same pattern
of prayer and release.

Now we are ready to look at the power of forgiveness and some
of the habit patterns that need to be broken. You are not who you
will be. You are on your way to becoming the real you—the person
God made you to be!

For Further Reflection

1. Explain the meaning of 2 Corinthians 5:17, that when you
   commit your life to Christ, old things pass away and all things
   become new.
2. What are the three parts of man?
3. What is the difference between eternal life and the fullness of
   salvation?
4. Why does a person need the ministry of both deliverance and
   healing in order to be made whole?
5. What are some of the indications that a curse is in operation?

10

Forgiveness and Breaking Destructive Habit Patterns

Joanne sobbed as she told me her story. She was a 49-year-old wife and the mother of three adult children. Her mother was in her seventies living about fifteen hundred miles away on the East Coast. Perhaps because the mother lived so far away, Joanne felt obligated to call her each day. On the other hand, Joanne could not remember a single day in her entire life that she had not talked to her mother—even on her honeymoon.

Memories of a life controlled by her mother tormented Joanne's mind. She felt she was at a breaking point in her life, yet she did not know the right thing to do, particularly as a Christian. The following questions plagued her:

- Aren't Christians supposed to love and honor their parents?

- The Bible says we are to submit to those in authority over us. Doesn't this include our parents?
- Is it wrong to want to live your own life when you are an adult?
- Am I being rebellious because I don't want to call my mother each day?[1]

Joanne was like many believers. The enemy used Scripture to deceive her and bring her into bondage. To be set free from the deception of entrapment by a controlling person and its associated pain, she needed to forgive her mother for years of control and manipulation, and then break the old habit patterns she exercised during the deception when she accepted her mother's control as biblical and right.

The apostle Paul had that same goal:

> Brethren, I do not regard myself as having laid hold of it yet; but one thing I do: forgetting what lies behind and reaching forward to what lies ahead, I press on toward the goal for the prize of the upward call of God in Christ Jesus.
>
> Philippians 3:13–14

For freedom to come to the believer, he or she must press through to forgiveness and press through to break old habit patterns in life.

Most of us desire to press on. We usually have a difficult time, however, in being able to forget what lies behind. To be free from the problems and pain of our past, and to be free from the consequences that continue to plague us, we must forgive. It is a decision we make to walk in a higher realm and receive the fullness of healing.

A person who has been deceived may have a root of unforgiveness or bitterness toward the person who deceived him or her: "See to it that no one comes short of the grace of God; that no root of bitterness springing up causes trouble, and by it many be defiled" (Hebrews 12:15).

If the deception has come through a church, leader or religious organization, the person may not have forgiven that individual or religious institution. (Can you forgive an institution? Yes!) The deceived person may even have unforgiveness toward God for not protecting him or her from the deception. Various other scenarios can cause unforgiveness in a person coming out of deception.

The Bad Fruit of Unforgiveness

I spend a lot of time in airplanes. At times the plane is flying at night or flying around storms. When I look out the window, I cannot see anything but black. During these dark times, I am thankful that the pilot does not trust what he is seeing or feeling in order to determine the direction the plane needs to fly. Instead he trusts the instruments to get the plane to its destination.

Christians should be the same way. We cannot look to our own feelings or understanding, since feelings or thoughts do not always tell us the truth. But bad fruit in a life means there is a bad root!

One of the ways we can recognize unforgiveness, then, is to look for bad fruit. Checking the fruit will determine if there is a root of bitterness or unforgiveness in the person's life.

Here are just three examples of bad fruit.

Mental Torment

Unforgiveness can cause mental torment. The Bible tells us that failure to forgive releases the person into the hands of tormenters (see Matthew 18:21–35). Often the unforgiveness produces bitterness and builds a wall of isolation around the person. The person retreats behind this emotional wall, distrusting others and fearful of further hurts. Loneliness fills his or her life. The person leaves a trail of broken relationships. There is little regret over cutting off others. Hardness and severity mark the person's life.

141

Defiling Others

The Bible says a root of bitterness will defile not only us but "many." Not only is the person affected but the bitter root also affects many others.

I read a story about a pastor who was asked to leave his church after a battle between him and the congregation. After leaving, this former pastor spent time trying to decide if he was going to continue to serve God or not. He finally decided to serve the Lord, and gathered a group of young people together. He portrayed himself through his teachings as God's "man of the hour" with God's "word of the hour." He was God's prophet with the word from the Lord.

The pastor did not deal with his root of bitterness over the fallout with his previous church. Many times a bitter spirit is like a spreading cancer. As a result, he gathered young people who were already bitter and had a root of bitterness—and the problem grew.

Over a period of time immorality began to take root. The group developed an evangelism tool called Flirty Fishing. Young people went out on the streets and seduced other young people to sleep with them. The practice of religious prostitution was used to show the *love of God*.

The bitterness that turned into immorality did not stop even at that point. A continual decline in biblical fidelity caused the group to move into deeper spiritual deception. That group is now one of the largest cults in the world, known as the Children of God. As time progressed, they became known as the Family of Love and have now taken the name The Family International, claiming members in more than one hundred countries.[2]

Where did it start? With bitterness and unforgiveness.

Sickness

A third fruit of unforgiveness is physical illness. People develop ulcers, high blood pressure, arthritis, migraines and many other

142

illnesses. Not all sickness is the result of unforgiveness, but many people suffer physical illness and are even hospitalized due to emotional hurts and unforgiveness.

The price is too high! Bad fruit is always the result of a bad root. Time does not wash away unforgiveness. Only confession and the blood of Jesus can do that. Failure to forgive will result in mental anguish, defilement of those around us and even physical illness.

Years ago I read a quote: "Everyone says that forgiveness is a lovely idea until they have something to forgive." It is true, forgiving is not easy. Grace is necessary in order to be able to forgive and extend mercy. Knowing that my own sins have been forgiven by the Lord, I can by God's grace forgive others.

Thoughts on Forgiveness

Following are some thoughts on forgiveness that may bring greater understanding so you can release the ones who hurt you.

Forgive so you can be forgiven. Jesus taught us to pray, "Forgive us our debts, as we also have forgiven our debtors" (Matthew 6:12). A person may not *feel* forgiveness at a deep level when he or she initially prays to release it. But the person will become able to forgive at a deeper level as the soul is healed. The more deeply we can forgive, the more we can receive joy, peace, power and love.

Ask God to make you willing. There are several levels of forgiveness that a person walks through on the path to freedom. Sometimes we forgive as a sheer act of the will. We forgive because Jesus commands us to forgive. When the task seems too great, it sometimes helps to ask God to make you willing. Be honest with the Lord. He knows your heart anyway.

Separate the person from the act. Forgiveness does not mean that we are condoning what the other person did. God never requires us to call wrongdoing or evil good. But we separate the deed from the person. Hate the wrong deed but forgive the person.

Forgive, regardless of reactions. Forgive when you do not know what the other person will do. My husband went to a couple to apologize for the hurt that he had caused them. He described the experience later as "throwing his hat into the ring." He said they not only stomped all over his hat but they threw it out the door! Even when your heart is right, the other person may not respond the way you think he or she will. Forgive anyway.

Forgive so you are not controlled. When you do not forgive, you will be controlled to some extent by that person. You refuse to go to a particular store or church if you think the other person may be there. You are being controlled and limited by the person who hurt you. When you forgive, you take away the weapons of the enemy.

Forgiveness is a decision. It is not a feeling. It is not pretending you were not hurt. You were! The pain is real. Yet you are making a supernatural decision to forgive genuine hurt and allow the Lord to heal you from your pain.

It is okay not to trust the person again. Forgiveness does not mean you have to trust the other person again. Trust is earned. When trust has been broken, it takes time to rebuild—and it does not always happen. Jesus did not trust everyone! "Jesus would not entrust himself to them, for he knew all men" (John 2:24, NIV). If Jesus did not trust everyone, He does not expect you to trust everyone either. Give yourself time to see if the person proves himself trustworthy.

Healing takes time. You will know you have forgiven the other person fully when you are able to wish him or her well; when you treat him or her as well as you do everyone else. You will no longer need to work at being kind. Your mind will no longer be filled with thoughts of what he or she did wrong. Healing takes time. Allow the Lord to continue to pour His love and forgiveness into your heart. Let Him be in your life what the other person is unable to be. Jesus' healing love is the strongest force in the universe!

Secrets for Breaking Free

For healing to occur in a person's life, there must be true repentance.

Some people think that crying and sorrow are signs of repentance. But true repentance means to have a change of mind. The mind is changed from evil to good or from worse to better. Regret and sorrow only bring oppression and remorse. True repentance brings release and freedom.

> The sorrow that is according to the will of God produces a repentance without regret, leading to salvation, but the sorrow of the world produces death.
>
> 2 Corinthians 7:10

A person can repent without tears. Repentance is a decision and not a feeling. When we change our minds, we will also change our actions. When we repent of unforgiveness and choose to walk in forgiveness, breaking old habit patterns that we developed in the past, we will ultimately have compassion and think differently about the person or situation that hurt us.

One of the first steps toward freedom is learning to stand in faith that you have indeed forgiven the other person.

Reckon as dead the offense that needed forgiving. You have forgiven the person, and now you declare that you will not give place to any unforgiveness in your life. Claim by faith that you are in the process of crucifying the old man. Refuse to allow yourself to feel, think, say or do anything that will resurrect unforgiveness.

We are born again by faith. We must also receive the work of the Spirit in our lives by faith. We do not trust our feelings. Feelings do not always tell the truth. Since you repented and forgave, the situation or person is forgiven!

The next step toward freedom and breaking old habit patterns is to recognize when times of testing come. These will follow repentance.

I remember praying for a friend I'll call John about forgiving his brother. He was excited about the release he felt during the time of prayer. After we finished praying, he walked outside and discovered his brother waiting for him. The old emotions erupted immediately.

John faced his test, he told me later, and determined to hold onto the victory he had just experienced. Recognizing his old patterns of temper and criticism, John resisted the habit of striking out at his brother in anger. He understood that if the ax is laid to the root, then the thing is dead. And because he recognized the time of testing, John refused to allow the recurrence of old habits to torment his mind and emotions and resurrect unforgiveness.

Those who, because of unbelief or a lack of self-discipline, refuse to do what John did can find their situation worse than it was previously.

> If, after they have escaped the defilements of the world by the knowledge of the Lord and Savior Jesus Christ, they are again entangled in them and are overcome, the last state has become worse for them than the first.
>
> 2 Peter 2:20

Self-discipline, as John exercised, is vital in recovering from the power of unforgiveness. The mind is the battleground where the victory is obtained. Every thought must be taken captive for healing to occur. Paul wrote that the weapons of our warfare are

> Casting down imaginations, and every high thing that exalteth itself against the knowledge of God, and bringing into captivity every thought to the obedience of Christ.
>
> 2 Corinthians 10:5, KJV

How do we do this?

Ignore Old Feelings

Old feelings will surface. Reject those feelings and resolve not to fight with them. Simply ignore them and realize they are not telling you the truth. In the same way that a ball, when dribbled, keeps on bouncing, ignore the ball. It will eventually stop bouncing when left alone.

Ignore Negative Thoughts

Our old thoughts do the same thing when they are ignored. So don't try to fight them. Concentrate on positive thoughts rather than the negative ones that attempt to enter your mind.

> Finally, brethren, whatever is true, whatever is honorable, whatever is right, whatever is pure, whatever is lovely, whatever is of good repute, if there is any excellence and if anything worthy of praise, dwell on these things.
>
> Philippians 4:8

Be Aware of the Lord

Another secret of breaking free is acknowledging the presence of the Lord on a continual basis. Things that are invisible are more real than the things that are visible. God is a Spirit. Angels are spirits. Although they are invisible, they are more "real" than the chair you are sitting on because they are eternal beings. Learn to be aware of the presence of the Lord at every moment. It will help you walk in a new level of grace and forgiveness.

I often tell people that Satan has won no victories in my life. Not that I have not sinned or made many mistakes! But I do not spend time talking or thinking about what the enemy has done to stop me. Rather, I make a practice of acknowledging that Jesus took the dung pile of my life and turned it into fertilizer. The fertile, workable soil of forgiven sin has caused me to grow into the person I am today. As grateful as I am for what God has done, I know He is not finished with me yet!

Laugh at Your Mistakes

Another secret to breaking old patterns is learning to laugh at your mistakes. Sometimes we as Christians think we are required to be perfect. Healing involves recognizing that our mistakes and failures do not make us unacceptable. In the school of the Spirit, they

147

are lessons that we learn along the way. Laughing at these mistakes brings us into healing. "A joyful heart is good medicine" (Proverbs 17:22). Take a humor break today and laugh at yourself! The Lord will take all the pain of your past and use it for ministry to others. Nothing is wasted in Him.

Don't Wait to Help Others

Most people want to wait until they are completely healed before helping others. Don't wait! Some of your healing occurs while you are helping others to be set free. If you have received only a teaspoon of healing, give the teaspoonful away to a hurting person. The Lord will then give you a tablespoonful. When you give the tablespoonful away, he will give you a cupful. Continue giving away what you have received until you are totally healed.

I do not remember where I read this quote by Etienne D. Grellet (1773–1855), but I wrote it down so I could remember this cry from my own heart: "I shall pass through this world but once. If, therefore, there be any kindness I can show, or any good thing I can do, let me do it now; let me not defer it or neglect it, for I shall not pass this way again." May this also be the cry of your heart as you walk in a new level of forgiveness and healing.

Get ready to break out of old habit patterns and receive a new anointing on your life for the new place!

Prayer

Heavenly Father, I come to You and acknowledge that You are Lord of my life. I confess that I have held unforgiveness in my heart. My mind has been filled with torment, anger, criticism and all sorts of evil thoughts. I hate these evil thoughts and the emotions that are associated with them. Please forgive me for harboring unforgiveness. I forgive myself for allowing unforgiveness to dwell inside me. I accept myself as a vessel of the Holy Spirit. I will not hate what You have created. Thank You, Lord, for forgiving me.

Lord, I choose to forgive [name the persons, situations or organizations]. I give [persons, situations or organizations] to You. I will not hold onto them any longer. I speak to [name of persons, situations or organizations] and I say, "I forgive you."

Lord, if there is any place of unforgiveness in my heart toward You, I ask for forgiveness. I realize that You are not my enemy. You are my deliverer. Thank You for cleansing me from all unforgiveness.

I ask You to give me the grace to break any old habit patterns in my life that are against Your will for me. Remind me when I am tempted to give life to wrong thoughts and emotions. With Your help, I will walk in a lifestyle of forgiveness. I will acknowledge Your presence. You are always with me. Thank You, Lord, for healing me and restoring the years that have been stolen from me. Thank You for complete victory and restoration in my life. In Jesus' name I pray, Amen.

For Further Reflection

1. What are some of the causes of unforgiveness?
2. What do we look for to determine if unforgiveness is lurking in our lives?
3. How do we forgive when there is no feeling of forgiveness? Is the forgiveness real?
4. What is required for unforgiveness to be cleansed from a person's life?
5. What are several ways to break old habit patterns in a person's life?

11

An Anointing to
Break You Out of Deception

The prophetic word of the Lord came to me during the worship service:

During this season, many of My people are tired and weary. They have been running but they do not feel that they have the strength to finish the race. The Lord says, "You are like the athlete who is running and does not feel he is able to complete the race. Yet the athlete receives a *second wind* that enables him to finish the race in victory. I am releasing a *second wind* to My Church during this season. As you catch the *second wind* of My Spirit, you will be able to complete your race in great victory!"

God's second wind is an anointing that believers need to complete their assignments from Him free from deception. The word *anoint* comes from a Hebrew root word meaning "to rub with oil . . . by implication, to consecrate; also to paint; smear."[1] The Holy Spirit wants to smear you with the oil of His presence so you can walk in the freedom Jesus purchased for you.

In biblical days, dried animal skins needed to be smeared and rubbed with oil. Sometimes the skins were used as containers for liquids. If the skins became dry and brittle, they broke. Dipping them in water, and then rubbing them with oil, kept them soft and pliable, extending their usefulness and value. These old wineskins, preserved, became new wineskins—no longer useless but valuable containers for new wine.

> "No one puts new wine into old wineskins; otherwise the new wine will burst the skins and it will be spilled out, and the skins will be ruined. But new wine must be put into fresh wineskins. And no one, after drinking old wine wishes for new; for he says, 'The old is good enough.'"
>
> Luke 5:37–39

Today God is rubbing His people with oil, anointing them, turning them into new wineskins to be used for His purposes.

The Breaker Anointing

The Lord is going to manifest the "breaker anointing" in the lives of these new wineskins who seek Him and His truth.

> "The breaker goes up before them; they break out, pass through the gate and go out by it. So their king goes on before them, and the LORD at their head."
>
> Micah 2:13

The breaker anointing is a supernatural empowerment by the Holy Spirit to experience victory in situations where we are not able to achieve victory on our own. The Breaker is not some spiritual goose bump; He is a Person—the Person of Jesus Christ. He rises up within the believer to break through every obstacle and hindrance that would keep you from your destiny.

Barbara Yoder wrote about the breaker anointing available for believers:

> The term "breaker" is foreign to most Christians. *Barnes' Notes* says that "Breaker-Through" is one of the titles given to Christ. The image here in Micah is one of both conquering and deliverance. Something has to be broken through; something has to be overcome. In Micah, the breaker crashes a gate in order to move the Israelites into the open place. It is a place where they are not confined. The gates of the prison—that which held them back—have been burst open to set them free. This is the same image found in Isaiah 43:6 when God speaks through Isaiah, "I will say to the north, 'Give them up!' And to the south, 'Do not keep them back.'"[2]

God is raising up a people today who are filled with the Spirit of the Lord. They have the Lord of the breakthrough on the inside of them. These people will reclaim their inheritance of freedom. They will face the enemy and break out of the imprisonment of deception and come into their inheritance of liberty and freedom.

Believers with the breaker anointing will function with the same anointing that fell on yielded men and women of God in the Bible. They did not force or imagine supernatural experience. They lived lives submitted to the Lord and were open to supernatural encounters when the wind of the Holy Spirit blew upon them:

> Prophecy never came by the will of man, but holy men of God spoke as they were moved by the Holy Spirit.
>
> 2 Peter 1:21, NKJV

The phrase *as they were moved* comes from a Greek term used in classical and New Testament literature. The term gives us a picture of a sailboat on the open water. Even though the sails are set to catch the wind, the vessel cannot move at will. It has to wait for the wind to blow and drive it, aided by the skill of the skipper, to its destination.

Peter is giving us a picture of the way we receive revelation, prophecy and supernatural manifestations. We do not force them, and must not concoct them, but simply prepare ourselves for the wind of the Spirit to blow on us and move us, carry us along, as He wills.[3]

Three things have to happen first.

Letting Go of Grief

Preparing for a fresh breaker anointing includes letting go of any grief from the last "season." Usually grief occurs when you have been deceived or when you have watched a trusted friend or associate fall into deception. To move into a new season with the Lord, you must release that grief. Grief will hold you in the old place. It will also cause you to forget your God-given destiny and vision.

The prophet Samuel had to deal with grief before he could receive a fresh anointing for himself and then be able to impart a fresh anointing to others for the new season:

> The LORD said to Samuel, "How long will you grieve over Saul, since I have rejected him from being king over Israel? Fill your horn with oil and go; I will send you to Jesse the Bethlehemite, for I have selected a king for Myself among his sons."
>
> 1 Samuel 16:1

Samuel was grieving the disobedience and sin in King Saul's life. Samuel was the one, after all, following God's leading, who had anointed Saul king. I am sure he had sustained great hope for God's purposes in and through that young man. Yet Saul fell into deception and never fulfilled God's best for his life. Now God was urging Samuel to let go of the grief and disappointment. He was encouraging Samuel to allow a fresh breaker anointing to break him out of the old season of Saul's deception and bring him into a new season of truth and freedom.

There are times when we put our trust in leaders. Some of these leaders we have trusted may fall into deception, and we are grieved. We see the potential they missed. We feel betrayed when they do not fulfill our expectations. We may experience the same emotions from the results of deception that we feel when a loved one dies. After all, in the case of the deceived person, we experience the death of trust and the death of potential in that person.

To move forward in freedom and receive a breaker anointing, however, you must deal with the grief. Grief will hold you in an old place.

Apprehending What the Lord Is Saying

Samuel was born at a time when there was no fresh prophetic voice to God's people. "Word from the LORD was rare in those days, visions were infrequent" (1 Samuel 3:1). Eli was a priest in a religious order that had no prophetic voice. Eli's sons were participating in immorality at the tent of meeting and making mockery of the Lord's offerings. Deception was rampant in the sons who were serving at the house of God.

So God removed the sons of Eli, who had forfeited their inheritance in the Lord, and raised up Samuel as a judge and prophet.

Samuel, in turn, was used to release a fresh breaker anointing on a young shepherd boy named David:

> Samuel took the horn of oil and anointed him in the midst of his brothers; and the Spirit of the LORD came mightily upon David from that day forward.
>
> 1 Samuel 16:13

Although God had sent His Spirit to rest on Saul, He now removed His Spirit from him. A new season had arrived. God would have a man "after His own heart" (1 Samuel 13:14) who would follow Him in truth. David's endowment with the Spirit "from that day forward" set him apart from Saul and Samson, upon whom the Spirit had descended only sporadically.[4] God's Spirit would now rest on David with an anointing to usher in a new season.

This new breaker anointing would also cause David to experience victory over his enemies:

> David came to Baal-perazim and defeated them there; and he said, "The LORD has broken through my enemies before me like the breakthrough of waters." Therefore he named that place Baal-perazim.
>
> 2 Samuel 5:20

Baal-perazim means *God of the breakthrough*. Believers can be empowered to walk in freedom from the enemy of deception. Our God of the breakthrough will break us out of the old place and launch us into a new season of truth.

Watchman Nee wrote about the anointing of the Holy Spirit and how it instructs the believer to walk free from deception:

> Anointing in the original signifies "applying ointment." This suggests how the Holy Spirit teaches and speaks in man's spirit. He does not speak thunderously from heaven nor does He cast the believer to the ground by an irresistible force. Rather does he work very quietly in one's spirit to impress something upon our intuition. In the same way that a man's body feels soothed when ointment is applied, so our spirit gently senses the anointing of the Holy Spirit. When intuition is aware of something, the spirit is apprehending what He is saying.[5]

Apprehending what the Lord is saying will release the breaker anointing upon us.

Declaring the Next Move of God

Allow God to release a prophetic declaration through you for your new season. Declare, "I am coming out of grief! I am coming into my new season of freedom!" You may not be a prophet but you are able to prophesy. The apostle Paul said that "you can all prophesy"

(1 Corinthians 14:31). So use your voice and prophesy that you are entering a new season of freedom.

God always raises up prophets at major intersections in history to break people out of the grief of the old season and to declare the next move of God.

Noah was a prophet. He was obedient to build an ark and proclaim a new season in the earth. Although there may never have been one drop of rain prior to the flood—although biblical scholars differ on this point—Noah prophesied a flood. He received supernatural revelation from God for the new season. Later prophets like Abraham and Moses also stood at major intersections in history and prophesied new moves of God in the earth.

We desperately need anointed prophets and prophetic people in the Church to receive revelation from God! We cannot throw away true revelation merely because we have experienced the false. True prophets are needed to keep the Church pure and to guard against the counterfeit.

I read a quote once that keeps me aware of the need for prophetic direction and revelation: "If you don't know where you are going, any road will get you there." How true that is! We need the anointing of God's Spirit to direct our paths in agreement with the truth of God's Word. Although I grew up in a church that told me prophets are not for today, how thankful I am for all the gifts, including prophecy, that Jesus gave His Church (see Ephesians 4:11–13).

We need true prophets in the Church to speak out and keep us free from deception, and also to declare the next move of God.

What Are the Results?

When do you need a breaker anointing? When something has been shut off in your life or when obstacles are limiting you from moving forward. A breaker anointing can actually push through and release you into your future. Psalm 29:5 tells us that the "voice of the LORD breaks the cedars; yes, the LORD breaks in pieces the cedars of Lebanon." The word *breaks* in Hebrew means "to burst, to break into pieces or to tear in pieces like a wild animal."[6]

Walking in freedom from deception requires an anointing that will be as violent in your spirit as a wild animal. This breaker anointing will destroy every remnant of deception in your life. It also provides a number of benefits for the person who is set free.

Receiving Your Inheritance

One of these benefits is the ability to receive the inheritance of the Lord. I read a story about a man who died after a lifetime of extreme poverty. After his death, a large bank account was discovered that had been left to him by his father. Although the money was his inheritance, he never knew it belonged to him. Consequently he spent his life in poverty.

Too many Christians live the same way. Jesus purchased an inheritance for His followers without limit, including forgiveness of sin, healing, prosperity, the gifts of the Spirit, fresh revelation, favor, miracles and a promised destiny. (Many more blessings of God are included in our inheritance, but this will give us a picture of what God has in store for those who are free to follow Him.) But the deception of religion, old mindsets, false religions, control, covenant-breaking, immorality, manipulation and other forms of deception have kept many Christians from receiving what belongs to them.

The Spirit of Revelation

Another benefit of the breaker anointing is the spirit of revelation:

I pray that the eyes of your heart may be enlightened, so that you will know what is the hope of His calling, what are the riches of the glory of His inheritance in the saints.

Ephesians 1:18

Many who have been caught in the trap of deception are fearful of new revelation after they have been set free. Trustworthy, loving mentors and leaders to whom they are accountable will confirm that revelatory insights are from God and help break them out of their fear and gain confidence.

My friend Barbara Yoder, senior pastor of Shekinah Christian Church in Ann Arbor, Michigan, known for her cutting-edge prophetic ministry, discusses the necessity of revelation in the life of a believer:

> Sometimes the thing holding us back is our failure to perceive spiritually. We have no revelation. One of the words for "hardness of heart" in Greek is *sklerokardia*, which means "destitute of spiritual perception." Our natural-mindedness must be broken through for revelation to be released. Without that breakthrough, our minds remain darkened. A veil blinds every Christian who fails to seek the Lord until revelation breaks through.[7]

Fresh revelation from God is not optional; it is essential.

Leaving the Old Behind

A third benefit of the breaker anointing is the change that begins to occur in the person's life. It is not enough merely to add new revelation to our understanding. We must leave behind the old mindsets, with their deception, for change to occur.

My husband, Dale, had an aunt who had trouble leaving old things behind. Years ago we were invited to her home to see her new sofa. Dale's dad warned me about what I would see when we arrived. He painted a good picture of Aunt Aileen's home. When we arrived, we saw exactly what I had been warned about. There was Aunt Aileen's new sofa. Next to it was the old sofa! She refused to let go of the old when the new arrived.

Believers have long thought that the old was good enough. They have been satisfied watching the professionals do the work of the ministry.

Today, however, God is raising up a people who want the new wine of the Holy Spirit. They are not content with the old mindsets and ordinary. They are recognizing that the Lord has a new anointing for them.

When our son, Mark, was two, he liked things to be done the same way every time. One day, when he arrived at his grandmother's house, he developed the same malady all children experience when they visit Grandma: extreme hunger. After Mark's grandmother placed him in a chair at the kitchen table, she prepared him a snack. She carefully spread peanut butter on crackers and put them on a plate. Mark picked up the first cracker and studied both sides. "The peanut butter is on the wrong side," he exclaimed. After all, I had always put the peanut butter on the opposite side of the cracker; anything different must be wrong.

We are often that way. We have definite ideas about what God does and does not do. Many of us think that only one side of the cracker can hold peanut butter, that only those involved in full-time ministry can have a breaker anointing. But God wants to smear the entire cracker!

Fresh Anointing

Today God is forming a new wineskin in His people—a wineskin made up of ordinary believers. He is releasing a fresh anointing on all who will receive, and they will be used to pour out the new wine of His Spirit, the new thing He is doing. Here is the cry from the hearts of this new wineskin: "The old is not good enough!" Along with the psalmist, they declare, "I have been anointed with fresh oil" (Psalm 92:10).[8]

This new breaker anointing breaks the yoke of deception and liberates God's people:

> "The Spirit of the Lord is on me, because he has anointed me to preach good news to the poor. He has sent me to proclaim freedom for the prisoners and recovery of sight for the blind, to release the oppressed, to proclaim the year of the Lord's favor."
>
> Luke 4:18–19, NIV

I often call this anointing the Fat Bull Anointing:

> So it will be in that day, that his burden will be removed from your shoulders and his yoke from your neck, and the yoke will be broken because of fatness.
>
> Isaiah 10:27

Most women do not like the word *fat*. They prefer words like *skinny, slim, trim, narrow* or *petite*. This is one time, however, that they will love the word *fat*! The word *fatness* often refers to grease, liquid or oil. But metaphorically it refers to a fat bull that has cast off its yoke and broken loose.[9]

The King James Version translates the word *fatness* as *anointing*.

> It shall come to pass in that day, that his burden shall be taken away from off thy shoulder, and his yoke from off thy neck, and the yoke shall be destroyed because of the anointing.
>
> Isaiah 10:27, KJV

God's people are going to become slippery and greasy in the anointing to break out of deception! They will get so fat in the anointing of God that they will break out of every yoke that has bound them. God will anoint them so powerfully that they will even help to radically break the yokes off others. They will be used by the Lord to deliver people out of the same trap that snared them.

Don't you just love the word *fat* in this sense? Don't you love the freedom the Lord has provided from all the deception of the enemy?

Your Spiritual Inheritance

A man I read about received an inheritance from his late father. After the paperwork had been filed, the funds were transferred to the man's bank account.

The man's father had been a rancher who spent many hard years working to buy land and equipment. He had a meager beginning

161

but knew how to plant the right crops at the right time. He was able to repair machinery and keep his equipment running longer than most ranchers. Through the years he managed to put a little money aside in order to leave a nice inheritance for his son.

Now the funds had been transferred to his son. Money that had previously been owned by his father became his. He was at liberty to take his newly acquired assets and invest them where they would multiply. By using wisely what he had received, he acquired, in a relatively short period, more than the sum of his father's lifelong endeavors. And his portfolio began with just a modest transfer.

Although you may think that your inheritance from your heavenly Father is modest, it will multiply and grow as you exercise faith in the deposit that has been made into your account. You have an inheritance of spiritual gifts—prosperity, joy, favor, relationships and many other benefits that Jesus purchased for you as one of His followers. As you receive and use the anointing that is given to you, it will increase. Just as this son received a transfer of funds from his earthly father, and increased his inheritance by wisely investing those funds, so you will see increase and multiplication in your life.

Go forth now in a fresh breaker anointing and make the enemy sorry he ever bothered you or those you minister to! Use your God-given inheritance to spread the Kingdom of God so that future generations will know the Lord and receive His blessings.

Prayer

Thank You, Lord, for providing a way for me to be set free. I choose to let go of all grief from the past season. I declare that I have an inheritance from the Lord and I will not be robbed of that inheritance by clinging to grief. I am Your sheep and can hear the voice of the Lord. I command my spiritual ears to open so that I can hear what You are saying to me.

Anoint me, Lord, with a fresh breaker anointing. I refuse

to live under the effects of deception any longer. Cause the Breaker to rise up within me and move me into my inheritance. I go forth with a fresh breaker anointing to see the captives set free and to see Your Kingdom increase! In Jesus' name, Amen.

For Further Reflection

1. Describe a time when you needed God's second wind to help you complete His assignment for you. What happened?
2. What is meant by the term *as they were moved* (see 2 Peter 1:21) when it was used in classical literature?
3. Why does the Church need prophets today?
4. Describe the effects of the breaker anointing.
5. How is the word *fatness* connected to the word *anointing*?

Conclusion

Maybe you have experienced a similar pattern in life as I have. I walked through many situations during my growing-up years that seemed to be merely disconnected events. Looking back, I now can "connect the dots" and see some of the big picture. Deception and deceptive doctrines have hovered near me throughout my life. I thought these doctrines and practices were unusual but did not understand their significance. I did not know that the enemy was behind these strange occurrences. Although I did not recognize the workings of the enemy at that time, I see more clearly now what was happening.

Like me, you are probably recognizing that things are no longer the same. Something has shifted in the realm of the Spirit. The eyes and ears of God's people have opened in a new way.

I remember when our daughter, Lori, was born. Her older brother, Brian, looked at her tiny body lying on the sofa. Her eyes, like those of most babies, were closed most of the time during those first few weeks. One day three-year-old Brian looked into her face and said, "Op your eyes, baby!"

I think that is what the Lord is saying to us. God is coming on the scene and calling His people to wake up to the dangers that are around them. He is alerting their spirits with a 911 warning.

Like Moses of old, a generation of people is arising who will challenge Pharaoh's magicians of this age. We are destined to demonstrate a power greater than the power of the deceiver. We will deliver a people out of the bondage of destruction. The Spirit of God on the inside of us, therefore, will not be silent. We will raise our voices like trumpets to call a people back to "the faith which was once delivered unto the saints" (Jude 3, KJV). We were born "for such a time as this" (Esther 4:14).

No longer will we be a people blown by every wind of doctrine that gusts through the earth. I remember attending seminars that painted pictures of some great big enemy coming for God's people. Christians were pictured as being so weak that the Lord had to rescue them or they would be destroyed. At first I had a hard time believing some of the things I was hearing, and felt as if those leaders must be watching too many science fiction movies. But listening to those teachings made me question my spiritual walk with the Lord. I finally concluded that those teachers were much more spiritual than I was since I could not embrace what they were saying.

Today we have learned through some of those experiences. We will no longer embrace the counterfeit spiritual experiences that do not glorify our precious Lord. We have been confused and disillusioned with strange fire that has not satisfied our deepest longings for the Lord. We are dissatisfied with much that has been offered in the name of the Lord. We will now contend for a genuine move of God's Spirit!

Our hearts are stirring with expectation for this fresh move of God. He is calling us to arise in sincerity, credibility, maturity and true holiness. We are living in a time when the world needs to see something genuine. They are waiting to see a people full of hope and faith. We can be those people.

I will never forget the first time I spoke at a meeting and the power of God was released. How surprised I was! People were healed. They received Jesus as Savior and were filled with the Spirit of the Lord. God somehow used me although I was not a Bible school graduate and was so new in the things of the Spirit. I was merely available to the Lord and wanted the new wine He was pouring out. God was more powerful than my own inadequacy.

Do not allow thoughts of inadequacy to hinder you from being used by God. He is preparing us to be new wineskins that can contain the pure wine of God's Spirit. This new wine is the true power of God!

My prayer for you is that you will hold fast to your faith in the Lord and His purpose for this generation. Do not shrink back from all that the Lord has planned for your life. Let Him use you to help bring a people out of darkness and into the fullness of His light. May the Lord use you to demonstrate His true supernatural power in the love and humility of God. God's best is not behind us. It is in front of us. Don't miss the best that God has for your life!

Appendix

A Solemn Prophetic Warning

The following prophecy has been in one of my files for more than twenty years.[1] I felt the time would come when I would write a book in response to the warning given by Stanley Frodsham. And now I have done so, to help prepare believers for the flood of deception being released in the earth. May my fellow believers be warned, prepared and equipped to be the victorious, glorious Church that overcomes the deception of the enemy!

Stanley Frodsham (1882–1969), born in England, became a leader in the Pentecostal outpouring of the early 1900s. For years he was the editor and publisher of all the Assemblies of God publications, ministering alongside early Pentecostal giants such as Smith Wigglesworth and Howard Carter. He wrote *Smith Wigglesworth: Apostle of Faith*, the classic biography of the British plumber who became a renowned international evangelist. Frodsham eventually separated from the Assemblies of God and began ministering among independent Pentecostals.

Out of a deep hunger for God, he was moved to give his early mornings and all nights to God in prayer. "I'm sure God has much for us," he said, "who will get desperate and spend much time waiting on Him." In 1964 the Spirit of God started to bring continual solemn prophetic warnings to him of coming delusion and error that would come to the churches. Frodsham warned of a spirit of deception descending on those who did not hold fast to the truth of the Bible and walk in holiness and righteousness.

Stanley Frodsham, known as God's "prophet with a pen," gave a sobering prophecy in 1965, warning of coming deception among believers. The text of that prophecy follows.

A Solemn Prophetic Warning

It is written: "Despise not prophesyings. Prove all things; hold fast that which is good" (1 Thessalonians 5:20–21, KJV). The following are excerpts from prophetic words given to one who was under a heavy anointing. We believe all who read these solemn prophetic warnings should take diligent heed to them. "Believe in the LORD your God, so shall ye be established; believe his prophets, so shall ye prosper" (2 Chronicles 20:20, KJV).

Great darkness is coming upon the countries that have heard My gospel but no longer walk in it. My wrath shall be manifested against all ungodliness. It shall come with great intensity. My judgments are literal, and not a thing to be lightly passed over. Before I visit the nations in judgment, I will begin at My house. When I do cause My wrath to come upon the cities of the world, My people shall be separate. I desire a people without spot or wrinkle, and such shall be preserved by Me in the time of My wrath coming upon all iniquity and unrighteousness.

I am going to prepare you for the coming days by a hard path that will cause you to cry out continually unto Me. For when the going is easy, men do not seek Me, but rejoice in a temporary blessing. And when that blessing is removed, they so often turn this way and that way, but do not come to Me. I am showing you these things that you may seek Me continually and with great diligence. As you seek Me, I will open up truths to you that you have not seen before, truths that will enable you to stand in the last days.

Coming Glory and Deceiving Spirits

When I visit My people in mighty revival power, it is to prepare them for the darkness ahead. With the glory shall come great darkness, for the glory is to prepare My people for the darkness. I will enable My people to go through because of the visitation of My Spirit. Take heed to yourselves lest ye be puffed up and think that you have arrived. Listen to the messengers, but do not hold man's persons in admiration. For many whom I shall anoint mightily with signs and miracles shall become lifted up and shall fall by the wayside. I do not do this willingly; I have made provision that they might stand. I call many into this ministry and equip them, but remember that many shall fall. They shall be like bright lights, and the people shall delight in them. But they shall be taken over by deceiving spirits, and shall lead many of My people astray.

Hearken diligently concerning these things, for in the last days shall come seducing spirits (1 Timothy 4:1) that shall turn many of My anointed ones away. Many shall fall through divers lusts and because of sin abounding. But if you will seek Me diligently I will put My Spirit within you (Ezekiel 36:27). When one shall turn to the right hand or to the left, you shall not turn with them, but keep your eyes wholly on the Lord. The coming days are the most dangerous, difficult and dark, but there shall be a mighty outpouring of My Spirit upon many cities; and many shall be destroyed. My people must be diligently warned concerning the days that are ahead. Many shall turn after seducing spirits; many are already seducing My people. It is those who do righteousness that are righteous. Many cover their sins by great theological words. But I warn you of seducing spirits who instruct My people in an evil way.

171

Many shall come with seducing spirits and hold out lustful entice-ments. You will find that after I have visited My people again, the way shall become more and more narrow, and fewer shall walk therein. But be not deceived, the ways of righteousness are My ways. For though Satan comes as an angel of light (2 Corinthians 11:13–15), hearken not to him; for those who perform miracles and speak not righteousness are not of Me. I warn you with great intensity that I am going to judge My house and have a church without spot or wrinkle when I come. I desire to open your eyes and give you spiri-tual understanding, that you may not be deceived, but may walk in uprightness of heart before Me, loving righteousness and hating every evil way. Look unto Me, and I will make you to perceive with the eyes of the Spirit the things that lurk in darkness that are not visible to the human eye. Let Me lead you in this way that you may perceive the powers of darkness and battle against them. It is not a battle against flesh and blood, for if you battle in that way, you ac-complish nothing. But if you let Me take over and battle against the powers of darkness, then they are defeated; and then liberation is brought to My people.

The Way of Deceivers

I warn you to search the Scriptures diligently concerning these last days, for the things that are written shall indeed be made manifest. There shall come deceivers among My people in increasing number, who shall speak forth the truth and shall gain the favor of the people, for the people shall examine the Scriptures and say, "What these men say is true." Then when they have gained the hearts of the people, then and then only shall they bring out these wrong doctrines. Therefore, I say that you should not give your hearts to men, nor hold people's persons in admiration. For by these very persons shall Satan enter into My people. Watch for seducers (1 Timothy 3:13). Do you think a seducer will brandish a new heresy and flaunt it before the people? He will speak the words of righteousness and truth and will appear as a minister of light, declaring the Word. The people's hearts shall be won; they will bring out their doctrines, and the people shall be deceived. The people shall say, "Did he not speak thus and thus? And did we not examine it from the Word? Therefore he is a minister of righteousness. That he has now spoken we do not see in the Word, but it must be right, for the other things he spoke were true."

Be not deceived, for the deceiver will first work to gain the hearts of many and then shall bring forth his insidious doctrines. You cannot discern those who are of Me and those who are not of Me when they start to preach. But seek Me constantly, and then when these doctrines are brought out, you shall have a witness in your heart that these are not of Me. Fear not, for I have warned you. Many will be deceived, but if you walk in holiness and uprightness before the Lord, your eyes shall be opened, and the Lord will protect you. If you will constantly look unto the Lord, you will know when the doctrine changes, and you will not be brought into it. If your heart is right, I will keep you, and if you will look constantly to Me, I will uphold you.

The minister of righteousness shall be on this wise: his life shall agree with the Word, and his lips shall give forth that which is wholly true, and it will be no mixture. When the mixture appears, then you will know he is not a minister of righteousness. The deceivers speak first the truth and then error to cover their own sins, which they love. Therefore, I exhort and command you to study the Scriptures relative to seducing spirits, for this is one of the great dangers of these last days.

I desire you to be firmly established in My Word, and not in the personalities of men, that you will not be moved as so many shall be moved. I would keep you in the paths of righteousness. Take heed to yourselves, and follow not the seducing spirits that are already manifesting themselves. Diligently inquire of Me when you hear something that you have not seen in the Word, and do not hold people's persons in admiration, for it is by this very method that Satan will hold many of My people.

The Way of Triumph

I have come that you might have life and have it more abundantly, that you may triumph where I triumphed. On the cross I triumphed over all the powers of Satan, and I have called you to walk the same path. It is when your life is on the cross that you shall know the victory that I have experienced. As you are on the cross and seated in Me, then you shall know the power of the resurrection. When I come in My glory, the principalities and powers in the heavenly places shall be broken. Fret not, for I have given you power whereby you may tread down the powers of darkness and come forth victoriously. It was on the cross that I triumphed over all the powers of the enemy.

My life shall flow through you as you enter into these precious truths. Look unto Me, and appropriate My life. As your eyes and desires are toward Me, and you know what it is to be crucified with Me, then you shall live, and your anointing shall increase. It was not in My life that I walked upon the earth, but it was in My life when I was upon the cross that I openly spoiled principalities and powers (Colossians 2:15). I am showing you truth that shall cause you to overcome, to have power over the wicked one—truth that will liberate you and those around you. You shall know also the fellowship of My sufferings. There is no other way whereby you may partake of this heavenly glory and reign with Me. "If we suffer, we shall reign with Him" (2 Timothy 2:12, kjv).

I desire to make these truths real within you. As you keep them before you, you will liberate many who are in bondage. You will have revelations of those in darkness and will have the keys to liberate the captives. Many seek to liberate, but they have not the keys. Upon the cross continually, you will know the power of My resurrection that you may also partake of My glory. As you are willing to walk with Me and rejoice in your sufferings, you shall partake of My glory. Look unto Me, for ye have need of power to overcome the wicked one and the bondage in other lives.

If you will indeed judge yourself, you shall not be judged (1 Corinthians 11:31). As you seek My face and desire to be cleansed by Me in all truth and sincerity of heart, I will judge you in the secret place, and the things that are in the secret place of your heart shall not be made manifest to others. I will do it in the secret place, and no man shall know it, and the shame that shall be seen on many faces shall not be seen on your face. Therefore, in love and mercy I am instructing you, and, therefore, have I said that if a man judge himself, he shall not be judged. It is not My good pleasure that the shame of My people be seen by all. How can I judge the world if I judge not first My own house? Hearken unto these things I am telling you. If you will not hearken to Me, your shame shall be evident to all.

God's Part and Our Part

I would have you consider My life on earth. The anointing upon Me was great. Yet the temptations were great on every side, in one form and then in another, offering Me first the glory of the kingdoms of the earth, and then reviling and persecuting Me. There will be great glory given to My people, and yet the temptations shall be intensified from every side. Think not that with the glory there shall be no temptations or persecutions. The glory to My Church shall be great, and so shall the temptations from the enemy to turn My people from My paths. I am warning you that when the glory shall be manifested, the temptations shall be great, until very few that start shall finish. First, there shall be offered them great worldly possessions, and then great revilings and unbelief.

Consider your Lord, that as He walked, so it shall be for you. There shall be need of great intensity of purpose. At times, everyone shall rise up against you, simply to turn you from the course that I would put you on. It is written of Me that I set My face as a flint to go the direction My Father had prescribed for Me (Isaiah 50:7). If you will finish the course the Lord has laid down for you, you will have to set your face as a flint with great determination. You must walk in the course laid down for you. Many of your loved ones and those who follow with you shall persuade you and try to turn you from the course. With many words that seem right in the natural will they speak to you. Did not Christ rebuke Peter, who would turn Him from the course God had prescribed (Matthew 16:22–23)?

Understand these two things and meditate upon them solemnly: the persecution and the darkness shall be as great as the glory, in order to try to turn the elect and the anointed ones from the path the Lord has laid down for them. Many shall start, but few shall be able to finish because of the greatness of grace that shall be needed to be able to endure unto the end. The temptation and persecution of your Lord was continuous. He was tempted by Satan in many forms throughout His entire life, and even on the cross when the ungodly cried out, "If thou be the Christ, come down from the cross." Think not that there shall be a time of no persecution, for it shall be from the time of your anointing unto the end—difficulties and great persecution to the end. The Lord must prepare you to be an overcomer in all things, that you may be able to finish the course. The persecution shall increase, even as the anointing shall increase.

In paths of judgment and righteousness shall the Lord God lead His people and bring them into that place which He has chosen for them. For the Lord has chosen a place for His people, a place of righteousness and holiness where He shall encamp round about them, and all who will be led of the Lord shall be brought into this holy place, for the Lord delights to dwell in His people and to manifest Himself through His people. The holiness of the Lord shall be manifested through His people. Let the Lord lead you in difficult places. He led His people of old through the place where no man dwelt, where no man had passed through—in a place of great danger, and in the shadow of death. The Lord will indeed lead His people through such places, and yet He will bring them out into a place of great glory. Understand that the way toward the glory is fraught with great danger, and many shall fall to the right or to the left; many shall camp on lesser ground, but the Lord has a place of holiness, and no unclean things shall dwell among His people.

Put your trust in Him, and He will bring you into a place of holiness. He desires to bring His people into great glory, the like of which has never been seen: what the Lord will do for those who put their trust in Him. It is a place of darkness and great danger that separates His people into the place He would have them walk in. He will protect them from the voices that would turn them from His path. He will bring them through the dark places, and through the treacherous paths, out into the light of His glory. He will rejoice greatly over His beloved, and cause you to be filled with joy unspeakable. He seeks to lead His people into a new place of grace and glory where He will indeed encamp among them. Put your trust in Him, and He will surely bring you into this new place.

Fear not the days to come, but fear this only: that you shall walk in a manner pleasing to the Lord. In this time I am ordering and setting up My church, and it shall indeed be pure, without spot or wrinkle. I will do a work in My beloved that has not been seen since the foundation of the world. I have shown you these things that you may seek the Lord diligently with all your heart, and that you may be a preserver of His people.

Run not to this one nor to that one, for the Lord has so ordained that salvation is in Him, and in Him alone. You shall not turn to this shepherd, or to that one; for there shall be a great scattering upon the earth. Therefore, look unto Him, for He will indeed make these things clear to you. You shall not look here nor there, for wells that once had water shall be no more. But, as you diligently seek Him, He shall increase your strength and your faith, that He may be able to prepare you for this time that is coming.

The truths that I have revealed to you must become a part of you, not just an experience, but a part of your very nature. Is it not written that I demand truth in the inward parts? It is the truth of the Lord expressed in your very being that shall hold you. Many shall experience the truth, but the truth must become a part of you—your very life. As men and women look upon you, they will hear not only the voice, but see the expression of the truth. Many shall be overcome because they are not constant in My ways, and because they have not permitted the truths to become part of them. I am showing you these truths that you may be prepared and, having done all, to stand.

Notes

Foreword

1. Francis Frangipane, *Discerning of Spirits* (Cedar Rapids, Iowa: Arrow, 1991), 6.

Chapter 1: Living in Perilous Times

1. Peter Marshall and David Manuel, *The Light and the Glory* (Tarrytown, N.Y.: Revell, 1977), 14.
2. Barbara Wentroble, *God's Purpose for Your Life* (Ventura, Calif.: Regal, 2002), 57.

Chapter 2: Be Not Deceived

1. Spiros Zodhiates, *Hebrew-Greek Key Word Study Bible, New American Standard Bible* (Chattanooga, Tenn.: AMG International, 2008), 1983.
2. Barbara Wentroble, *Prophetic Intercession* (Ventura, Calif.: Regal, 1999), 58–59.
3. Barbara Wentroble, *Praying with Authority* (Ventura, Calif.: Regal, 2003), 138–39.

Chapter 3: Lying Signs, Wonders and Apparitions

1. Rick Renner, *Merchandising the Anointing* (Tulsa: Rick Renner Ministries, 1990), 15.
2. http://skepdic.com/firewalk.html.
3. Renner, *Merchandising*, 153.

Chapter 4: Seducing Spirits and Doctrines of Demons

1. John McCoy, "The Fear of Demons: The Death of a Child, Mother Awaits Murder Trial in Slaying of Girl," *Seattle Post-Intelligencer*, April 10, 1986.

2. William M. Alnor, "Research Notes: Bernie Siegel, Donald Lee Barnett," *Christian Research Institute Journal*, April 25, 2003.

3. *A Dictionary of World History*, s.v. "Muhammad," http://www.encyclopedia .com.

4. http://www.christadelphia.org/belief.htm.

5. http://www.brittanica.com/EBchecked/topic/269257/Holiness-movement.

6. *Webster's Dictionary*, (1913), s.v. "Montanists."

7. *The Oxford Dictionary of Phrase and Fable* (Oxford University Press, 2006), s.v. "Albigenses" (by Elizabeth Knowles), http://www.encyclopedia.com.

8. *The Columbia Encyclopedia, 6th ed.*, s.v. "Beghards," http://www.bartleby.com /651.

9. Ed Margaret Drabble, "Ranters," *The Oxford Companion to English Literature*, (Oxford University Press, 2000), http://www.enotes.com/oce-encyclopedia/ranters.

10. *The Columbia Encyclopedia*, s.v. "John Humphrey Noyes," http://www.encyclo pedia.com.

11. http://mormonmatters.org/2008/06/03/mormon-ancestor-worship/.

12. Renner, *Merchandising*, 47.

13. Ibid., 116–17.

14. I have had this prophecy in my files for more than twenty years, and no longer remember the source or how I received it. However, the prophecy is available in various places on the Internet, including http://www.nonprofitpages.com/elm7/ frodsham.htm.

Chapter 5: Judging the Supernatural

1. Zodhiates, *Study Bible*, 2157.

2. Watchman Nee, *The Latent Power of the Soul* (New York: Christian Fellowship, 1972), 20–21.

3. http://charismamag.com/index.php/newsletters/fire-in-my-bones/18454-strange-fire-in-the-house-of-the-lord.

4. Renner, *Merchandising*, 11–13.

Chapter 6: Guarding against Deception

1. Ruth Specter Lascelle, *A Dwelling Place for God* (Seattle: "Wuffy" Ruth Bagaas, 1973), 191–94.

2. Paul Vitello, "For Catholics, A Door to Absolution Is Reopened," *New York Times*, February 10, 2009, http://www.nytimes.com/2009/02/10/nyregion/10indulgence .html?_r=1&ref=us&pagewanted=print.

3. Renner, *Merchandising*, 196.

4. http://www.forerunner.com/eschatology/X0011.Postmil.html.

5. Ted W. Engstrom, *The Fine Art of Mentoring* (Brentwood, Tenn.: Wolgemuth & Hyatt, 1989), 3–4.

6. Barbara Wentroble, *Rise to Your Destiny, Woman of God* (Ventura, Calif.: Regal, 2006), 103.

Chapter 7: Dangers of Passivity and Spiritual Boredom

1. Renner, *Merchandising*, 89–90.

2. Vinson Synan, "The Origins of the Pentecostal Movement" (Tulsa: Holy Spirit Research Center, Oral Roberts University), http://www.oru.edu/university/library/holyspirit/pentorg1.html.

Chapter 8: Deceptive Practices through History

1. Nee, *Latent Power*, 21.

2. Spiros Zodhiates, *The Hebrew-Greek Key Study Bible, New American Standard, Lexical Aid to the New Testament* (Chattanooga: AMG International, 1990), 1816.

3. Renner, *Merchandising*, 116–17.

4. http://ezinearticles.com/?Corruption-Of-The-Church-In-The-Middle-Ages&id=969734.

5. "Triumph of the Cross," *Modern Liturgy*, September 1997), 1.

6. http://en.wikipedia.org/wiki/Stigmata.

7. http://www.assap.org/newsite/articles/Stigmata.html.

8. Ibid.

9. http://www.willingshepherds.net/.

10. http://www.telegraph.co.uk/news/worldnews/1567216/Italy%27s-Padre-Pio-%27faked-his-stigmata-with-acid%27.html.

11. http://www.vivendodaluz.com/EN/amboflight/theresa_neumann.html.

Chapter 9: Deliverance and Healing

1. Bronwen Healy, *Trophy of Grace* (Brisbane, Australia: Desktop Publishing, 2004), 260.

2. *Vine's Expository Dictionary of New Testament Words* (Westwood, N.J.: Barbour, 1952), 316.

3. Derek Prince, *Blessings and Curses* (Grand Rapids: Chosen, 2003), 12–15.

4. Ron G. Campbell, *Free from Freemasonry* (Ventura, Calif.: Regal, 1999), 13, 36–37, 62–63.

5. Barbara Wentroble, *Freedom from Deception* (Keller, Tex.: Palm Tree, 2008), 32.

Chapter 10: Forgiveness and Breaking Destructive Habit Patterns

1. Wentroble, *Purpose*, 124.

2. Wentroble, *Deception*, 21–22.

Chapter 11: An Anointing to Break You Out of Deception

1. Kelly Varner, *Understanding Types, Shadows and Names*, vol. 1 (Shippensburg, Pa.: Destiny Image, 1996), 45.

2. Barbara Yoder, *The Breaker Anointing* (Ventura, Calif.: Regal, 2004), 25–26.

3. Renner, *Merchandising*, 164–65.

4. Luder Whitlock Jr., *New Geneva Study Bible* (Nashville: Thomas Nelson, 1995), 391.

5. Watchman Nee, *The Spiritual Man*, vol. 2 (New York: Christian Fellowship, 1968), 74.

6. Zodhiates, *Study Bible*, 1780.

7. Yoder, *Breaker*, 33.

8. Barbara Wentroble, *You Are Anointed* (Ventura, Calif.: Regal, 2001), 28–29.
9. Ibid., 147.

Appendix

1. As mentioned previously, I have had this prophecy in my files for more than twenty years, and no longer remember the source or how I received it. However, the prophecy is available in various places on the Internet, including http://www.nonprofitpages.com/elm7/frodsham.htm.

Index

parents, honoring of, 65–66
passivity, 100–109
patience, 47
Paul
  on deception, 29, 57
  discernment of, 51, 53
  on false teachers, 115–16
  on freedom, 140
  on heaven, 67
  on judging, 72–73
  on law, 94
  on spiritual gifts, 106
  on spiritual warfare, 121
peace, 143
Pentecost, 109
Pentecostals, 107, 168
perceptions, 37
personality, 82
Peter, 49–50, 52, 78–79
Pharisaism, 94
physical illness, 142–43
Pio, Padre, 119–20
"police gift," 78
poverty, 132
power, 112–14, 143
prayer, and emptying of mind, 57
presence of God, counterfeit, 48–49
pride, 82, 93, 135
priests, believers as, 89
Prince, Derek, 130
prophesy, 73, 156–57
Protestant Reformation, 91
Protestants, 107
Psychic Channels (TV show), 22
psychoanalysis, 38
psychotherapy, 64

quiet spirit, 101–2

Ranters, 63
rebellion, in heaven, 41
reincarnation, 64, 102
relationship, 108
relics, 116–17
Renner, Rick, 46, 50, 92–93, 103, 116
repentance, 19, 145
restoration, 122
revelation, spirit of, 158–59
Roman Catholicism, 91, 118

salvation, 19
  as process, 127–28
Samuel, 154–55
sanctification, 52, 127–28
Satan, 17, 27
Saul, 154
seducing spirits, 57–58
self-discipline, 146
self-help, 64
sexual assault, 57
sickness, 142–43
signs and wonders, 108
Simon the sorcerer, 51–52
sin, as deceitful, 35
Smith, Joseph, 49
sorcery, 113
soul, 74
"soulical" connections, 56
spirits, 38–39, 74
  discernment of, 37–38, 77–79
  testing of, 73–74
spiritual gifts, 41, 106, 162
spiritual metaphysics, 38
spiritual sight, 50–51
spiritual warfare, 121–22
stigmata, 45, 47, 117–21
strange fire, 90
style, 82

Taoism, 75, 114
teachers, as deceived, 59
Therese of Lisieux, 120
tithing, 134–35
trust, 144
truth, 30, 48
  discerning, 88–89

ultimate reconciliation, 18
"unauthorized fire," 81
unforgiveness, 93, 140–43
United States, Christian principles of, 22
Urim and Thummim, 89

virgin Mary, 43–44, 48, 119
visionaries, 43
visions, 13, 50
visitations, 14
voices, of deception, 19–20

Barbara Wentroble, mother, wife and entrepreneur, is a strong apostolic leader gifted with a powerful prophetic anointing. She has motivated and coached leaders in all spheres of influence: government, business, education, media and more. Her goal is to unlock your gifts and catapult you into realizing your potential as a reformer in your sphere of authority. She provides practical teachings to apply to your life, giving you a formula for success. Her wisdom and straightforwardness are part of the package, but her faith is the true ingredient to take you to the top.

Barbara's pioneering spirit is evident through her cutting-edge teaching and impartation that releases God's purposes. A powerful breakthrough anointing is released as she ministers. She activates giftings and anointings in ministers, business leaders and individuals.

Barbara is founder of International Breakthrough Ministries (IbM), an apostolic network that unites business leaders and church leaders for opportunities in the Kingdom of God. This alliance provides an atmosphere to develop covenantal relationships with strategic visionaries.

Barbara is also president of Breakthrough Business Network (BBN). BBN provides spiritual accountability, and it encourages, validates and promotes an environment of integrity and success for Kingdom businesses.

Barbara has written several other books, including *Rise to Your Destiny, Woman of God*; *Prophetic Intercession* and *Praying with*

Authority. She is a frequent contributing author for several Christian magazines.

Barbara and her husband, Dale, live in Dallas, Texas. They are the parents of three adult children and eight grandchildren.

For more information about International Breakthrough Ministries, for booking information, to subscribe to e-news or for product orders, please contact:

International Breakthrough Ministries
P.O. Box 2208
Coppell, TX 75019
(972) 870-0208 (phone)
(972) 753-0208 (fax)
email: ibm@internationalbreakthroughministries.org
website: www.internationalbreakthroughministries.org

Barbara Wentroble, President

Ways to connect with IbM

Fellowship Associate

For those who want to connect with IbM on an ongoing basis and support it financially.

Executive Network

Comprised of visionary marketplace and ministry leaders who are equipped to bring cutting-edge transformation to their spheres of influence.

IbM Intercessors

For more information on local meetings and conference call intercession, contact Falma Rufus at the IbM office.

For more information and to learn more about International Breakthrough Ministries, please visit our website at www.internationalbreakthroughministries.org.
For booking information, subscribe to e-news and product orders, please contact us at:

International Breakthrough Ministries
P.O. Box 2208
Coppell, TX 75019
972-870-0208 – Office
972-753-0208 – Fax
ibm@internationalbreakthroughministries.org

Breakthrough Business Network provides meaningful relationships that facilitate spiritual oversight, education and motivation for convergence with Kingdom goals.

For more information and to learn about Breakthrough Busness Network, please contact our office or visit our website at www.breakthroughbusinessnetwork.com.

3001 Gateway Dr, Suite 105
Irving, TX 75063
972-870-8767
bbn_office@sbcglobal.net